Life, as we all know, is filled with disappointments; however, no emotion is more piercing than that of a betrayal from a so-called friend. To walk in peace, harmony, and the joy of the Lord, a person must understand Satan's strategy of betrayal and mistrust. In his new book, *Betrayed*, Pastor Randy Valimont uses Scripture, word studies, and personal stories to give the reader insight and necessary tools to overcome any form of disappointment through betrayal. No one understood betrayal better than Christ, whose own disciple, Judas, turned against Him for thirty pieces of silver. Don't just read this book but put into practice this content, and you can learn to overcome and walk in complete victory.

—PERRY STONE
Founder, Voice of Evangelism and host of *Manna-Fest*

My friend Randy Valimont, like a trained physician during an examination, has placed his hand on the body of Christ where we hurt the most. The pain of betrayal is so great that it causes the strongest among us to faint. As I read the manuscript, I felt that every chapter was like a prescription from heaven's apothecary, which brings healing that only the Holy Spirit can bring.

—JOHN KILPATRICK
Founder, Church of His Presence
Facilitator, Brownsville Revival

The subject of betrayal is explained by author Randy Valimont to lie at the core of humanity's greatest disasters. Valimont provides incredible substantiation for what is truly no argument—betrayal was evident from the azure halls of heaven, where Satan betrayed the magnificence of the Almighty, to the cobblestone streets of Jerusalem, where the Son of the Almighty Himself paid the price for all of our betrayals. *Betrayed* is one of the most outstanding reads dealing with human nature's most outstanding needs. Kudos to Pastor Valimont for tackling this sensitive subject with solutions that resolve this human flaw through the grace of God.

—DAVE ROEVER, DD
Evangelist, Roever & Associates

Pastor Randy Valimont has written a very important book. *Betrayed* will touch the hearts of many who need healing. This book is real. It is riveting and difficult to put down. God bless you, Randy, for sharing this important book with us.

—JIM BLANCHARD
Chairman of the board, Synovus (financial institution)

This superb, refreshing, and thought-provoking book shines a piercing light on the schemes of the enemy and is deeply needed! *Betrayed* has something to be learned by people in all walks of life, no matter what your church, socioeconomic background, or culture. It is a must-read!

—DR. TIM TODD
President/executive director, Revival Fires International

One of the most wounding experiences in life and ministry is to be betrayed by someone you trust. Betrayal need not make you bitter, however. With God's help, you can become better. In *Betrayed* my friend Randy Valimont shows how.

—DR. GEORGE O. WOOD
General superintendent, General Council of
the Assemblies of God

After years of pastoral ministry, there is no one better suited than Pastor Randy Valimont to convey the magnanimous truths found in this book. Many people have experienced betrayal in their lives and ministries. Often those situations were hard to understand. However, through experience I have found that God vindicates, and one's attitude is important through every trial and circumstance. If you have experienced betrayal, the content of this book will be a source of encouragement and strength. The chapter on healing from the effects of betrayal is filled with truth as it points out that we must trust God with our sorrows and the uncertainties of life. Regardless of your pain, heartache, and sorrow, this book will encourage you to not be controlled by circumstances but to remain faithful to God's calling and His plan for your life.

—Rev. (Dr.) Huldah Buntain
President, Assembly of God Mission
Calcutta, India

If you haven't been betrayed then you've never been in church leadership. It is not a matter of *if*, it's a matter of *when*. The biggest challenge is that protecting yourself against betrayal robs you of your ability to help with vulnerability. The moment people can't hurt us is the moment we stop helping. Betrayal is that part of life that even our Lord wasn't able to escape. In *Betrayed* my friend Randy Valimont describes the nuances and faces of betrayal, but most of all he helps us understand our responses to the same. This is one issue you will not and cannot escape in leadership—you'd might as well be prepared. Pastor Valimont will equip you well. This is a must-read for every church leader.

—Dr. Sam Chand
Leadership consultant
Author, *Cracking Your Church's Culture Code*
www.samchand.com

BETRAYED

BETRAYED

RANDY VALIMONT

CHARISMA
HOUSE

BETRAYED by Randy Valimont
Published by Charisma House
Charisma Media/Charisma House Book Group
600 Rinehart Road
Lake Mary, Florida 32746
www.charismahouse.com

Biblica, Inc.™ Used by permission of Zondervan. All rights reserved worldwide. www.zondervan.com. The "NIV" and "New International Version" are trademarks registered in the United States Patent and Trademark Office by Biblica, Inc.™

Scripture quotations marked THE MESSAGE are from *The Message: The Bible in Contemporary English*, copyright © 1993, 1994, 1995, 1996, 2000, 2001, 2002. Used by permission of NavPress Publishing Group.

Cover design by Justin Evans
Design Director: Bill Johnson

Visit the author's website at www.griffinfirst.org.

Library of Congress Control Number: 2014936503
International Standard Book Number: 978-1-62136-034-6
E-book ISBN: 978-1-62136-035-3

First edition

14 15 16 17 18 — 9 8 7 6 5 4 3 2 1
Printed in the United States of America

It has been said that if we see a turtle on a fence post, someone must have put him there. I dedicate this book to some of the many people who put this turtle on all the fence posts God has blessed me to stand on.

To my dear, lovely wife, Jelly, who has walked with me through numerous betrayals—you have helped me grow from an arrogant, insecure young man to (I hope) a more secure man, who isn't nearly as arrogant. Your love, compassion, and strength have been a part of every message, every counseling session, every leadership seminar, and each book, especially this one.

To my children, Jordan, Danielle, and Alayna—you are literally the best daughters any father could ever have. You make me proud, and you make me pray. You laugh at me and with me. You encourage me and give me perspective that sometimes I don't enjoy without your help. I love you dearly.

To my son-in-law, Chris—I am proud of the way you have overcome betrayals in your life with strength, dignity, and honor. I couldn't love you any more or be any prouder if you were my own son.

And to my beautiful granddaughter, Jaeli—you are special beyond words and bring us all so much joy. Grow up, change the world, challenge the world, and take charge of the world.

Finally, to my pastor of forty years, Fred Richard, who leads Northwood Assembly in Charleston, South Carolina—your strength, courage, wisdom, faith, and godly example helped me stay the course and fight the fight when at times I wanted to run.

I thank you all for the shared visions, dreams, and goals.

CONTENTS

ACKNOWLEDGMENTS

HAD THE PRIVILEGE of sitting on the board of Southeastern University when Dr. Mark Rutland was president. He made a statement during one board meeting that has stuck with me through the years: "Whenever you see a turtle sitting on a fence post, you know that he didn't get there by himself; he obviously had a lot of help."

I would not have had the ability to write this book without the generous help and support of my dear wife, Jelly. Together, we spent hours going over the manuscript, along with the fine folks at Charisma House.

I would be remiss if I didn't thank all of those who were so generous to endorse the book. All of these are dear friends who have been a blessing to me in so many ways. I would also like to thank a group of men who have been so supportive of this effort. The official board of Griffin First Assembly allowed me the time to take on this project and were supportive throughout the process.

A special thanks goes to my assistant, Deborah Rabern. Life would not function without her support and help. This project added one more thing to her plate, and she never complained.

I would also like to thank my family and friends who were so clear in their support during the difficult days of the betrayals we faced. Their prayers and intercession on my behalf is why this book has made it into your hands.

Last but not least, I want to thank you for having the courage to purchase and read this book. I believe it will encourage you and help you finish the race well. I understand that we get nothing without the Holy Spirit and His help in our lives, and that goes double for me. He is the one who gives us strength and wisdom as we walk through betrayal.

Be blessed and remember, betrayal doesn't define us; it only opens a door to the miraculous.

It is not an enemy who taunts me—I could bear that. It is not my foes who so arrogantly insult me—I could have hidden from them. Instead, it is you— my equal, my companion and close friend.
—PSALM 55:12–13, NLT

INTRODUCTION

I N THE SIXTIES the United States went to war with Vietnam. Many of our young men were drafted to serve in this war, and almost 60,000 US soldiers gave their lives for our country. Because of the controversy surrounding whether America should have engaged in this conflict at all, many of the soldiers were denied a hero's welcome upon returning home. They were spit on, mocked, and even called "baby killers." There were no parades; there was ridicule. The veterans were ostracized, and many ended up homeless, disillusioned, and battling post-traumatic stress disorder without support. They checked out of Vietnam and then out of society in general, feeling betrayed by both the American public and the US government.

As if their lackluster homecoming were not enough, years later it was proved that while in Vietnam, US soldiers were exposed to a type of chemical warfare known as Agent Orange. Many died as a result. Recent research has even found possible links between Agent Orange and some cases of cancer, diabetes, and Parkinson's disease in veterans, as well as certain birth defects in children of veterans.[1]

Two of my dear friends who served in Vietnam have suffered the physical side effects of Agent Orange exposure, and both of their wives died of breast cancer. One of the men often has said that it took him a long time to return to the United States emotionally. He'd put his life on the line for the country he loved, but he felt betrayed at the reception he received upon his return home. He was shown no honor or appreciation for his service. The anger and resentment has subsided over time, but even now his eyes moisten with tears when he discusses the war with other vets. Betrayal hurts.

Sadly, betrayal is hardly a rare occurrence. In the seventies the American public was betrayed when it was proved that President Richard Nixon was involved in covering up a break-in at the Watergate offices of the Democratic National Committee. Betrayal rocked the church world the following decade when the moral and financial failures of several high-profile televangelists were exposed.

In the nineties Bill Clinton, former president of the United States, lied under oath to congressional leaders about having an affair with a former White House intern. Clinton's affair with Monica Lewinsky not only cast a large shadow on the integrity of every politician, it also led to a reported increase in oral sex among high school students. One of the high school students in our church even told his parents that he did not understand why they were making such a big deal about his engaging in this activity. If President Bill Clinton did it, he wondered, why couldn't he? This shows how the ripple effects of betrayal can affect families, churches, and even a nation.

Political candidates make promises they cannot and do not intend to keep. Students turn in assignments that they have plagiarized. Parents do their children's homework. Business and civic leaders deliberately deceive their shareholders and constituents. We even see ministers lying about successes in their ministries: the size of the congregation, the health of their finances, and so on. There seems to be an idea that if you do not get caught in a lie, it is not really a lie.

Future employees invent work histories on their employment applications. One famous example was George O'Leary, the former football coach at Georgia Tech. After Notre Dame University hired him as their coach, they discovered he had been untruthful about his academic accomplishments.[2] What would have been his dream job became a nightmare when he was forced to resign because of his deception. Both the university and its alumni felt betrayed.

Betrayal often occurs in the area of finances as well. Bernie Madoff purported to be a great financier. He seemed to have great success and attracted a large, impressive client list. At one point in time his firm was responsible for handling up to 5 percent of the trading on the New York Stock Exchange. But in late 2008 Madoff's sons reported him for securities fraud. Madoff admitted to the authorities that one branch of his business was actually an elaborate Ponzi scheme. He pled guilty to eleven felony counts of securities fraud, investment advisor fraud, money laundering, false statements, perjury, and false filings with the United States Securities and Exchange Commission. He admitted that he had lost $50 billion of investors' money and was sentenced to one hundred fifty years in prison, a maximum sentence for his crimes.[3]

Lying and deception have become commonplace in our culture today. People do not seem to mind deceiving others when it benefits them, but no one likes to feel the sting of betrayal. Unfortunately you can't have one without the other. Lying and deception are at the root of betrayal because deception breaks trust and betrayal is broken trust.

Benedict Arnold is well known for his act of treason during the Revolutionary War—so much so that his name has become synonymous with betrayal. But many people do not know that he was once a hero for the United States and a military genius. In fact, we probably would not have won the Revolutionary War without his military prowess.

Born in Connecticut, Benedict Arnold rose to the ranks of general in the Continental Army. He was successful in many of his battles and believed so strongly in the Continental cause that he funded some of its efforts with his own money. But history tells that other officers claimed credit for his successes, and Arnold was passed over for promotion many times. His lack of promotion caused Arnold to become angry and bitter. He began to make enemies and eventually was considered a divisive figure.

In 1775 he returned home after battle and found that his wife, Margaret, had died and left him to raise their children on his own. Perhaps this was the proverbial straw that broke the camel's back. After giving so much for his country, he received no recognition and then he lost his wife while he was away at war. In 1780 he colluded with the British to surrender the fort of West Point. Arnold's plot was discovered and thwarted and, evading arrest for treason, he began to openly fight for the British army. After the war ended, he moved to London, where he died at the age of sixty. Arnold may have regretted his treasonous acts against his country, but his one act of betrayal became his legacy.[4]

Betrayal is not limited to historical figures, of course. Most people know how it feels to be betrayed socially, spiritually, or financially; in friendship, through a family member, in the workplace, in the church, and even through a spouse. The question to ask is not, "Have you ever been betrayed?" but, "*How* have you been betrayed?"

We live in a culture where betrayal is epidemic. Because betrayal comes in many different forms, it can inflict different kinds of hurt and pain. The depth of our emotional commitment to the person or situation will determine the depth of pain we will experience from a betrayal. Some betrayals may hurt only a little while others can be debilitating.

In many ways our culture is being shaped by betrayal. According to sociologists, every generation will leave an imprint on our culture. That imprint will affect future generations. The Greatest Generation (born between 1901 and 1924) gave our nation a hard work ethic and strong financial stewardship because they lived through the Great Depression and served in World War II. They taught us perseverance, sacrifice, honor, duty, and faith. The current generation is leaving an imprint of betrayal with its tolerance for deception.

Today betrayal seems to be at the forefront of every newspaper article, with report after report about child molestation, murder, divorce, infidelity, abuse, stock fraud, and so on. Because betrayal can inflict such deep wounds, it can leave us permanently scarred. If we don't deal with betrayal in a healthy way, it can even derail our future. Satan would like nothing more than for you to let betrayal keep you from trusting others or from embracing the people God puts in your life. He would love to see you let bitterness destroy your life and relationships.

But there is hope. Not only is there life after betrayal, but also God is able to work the experience together for your good. In the pages of this book I will explain how to find healing from the effects of betrayal and move forward with God's plan for your life. I will also explain how to identify a betrayer so you can possibly avoid future hurt. As we walk this journey together, using Jesus as our role model, it is my hope that the Lord will cause our weaknesses to become strengths, turn our sorrows to joy, and use the betrayals we experience to make us better—for one another, for ourselves, and most importantly, for the kingdom of God.

Chapter 1

THE GENESIS OF BETRAYAL

Y OU TOO, BRUTUS?" Those are the famous words Julius Caesar spoke as he looked at the senators surrounding him with swords. He had begun to resist the assassination until he scanned the group and saw that his dear friend, Marcus Brutus, was among his betrayers. If you've ever been betrayed, you can imagine the hurt Caesar felt. The wounds of betrayal run deep.

Throughout my thirty-plus years of ministry, I have done a variety of counseling. I have found that most of the problems people encounter are centered in some form of betrayal—someone spent money that should have been saved. Someone made a comment that should not have been said. Someone broke a trust and brought heartache and pain.

When in the middle of the crisis it is hard to understand how someone we love or trust could inflict so much hurt. We ask ourselves how sin entered our home, church, or relationship. We wonder what we did to deserve such pain.

In reality it is highly unlikely that you did anything to warrant the betrayal. You are not paying a price for some unknown seed you have sown. To fully understand why betrayal occurs, we must take a look back at the genesis of betrayal.

Betrayal started in the most unbelievable of all places: heaven. God created three archangels at the beginning of time. The first was named Gabriel. He was known as the messenger angel because in biblical times whenever there was an important message to be sent, Gabriel was the one who delivered it. Gabriel, for instance, is the one who told Mary she would conceive of the Holy Spirit and give birth to the Son of God (Luke 1:26–33).

The second angel was named Michael. He was the warring angel. Whenever God sent destruction, Michael was the one to go forth and draw his sword. He was the prince of warriors, as noted in Daniel 12:1, "At that time Michael shall stand up, the great prince who stands watch over the sons of your people."

The third archangel was named Lucifer. He was the worshipping angel. Lucifer's job in heaven was to create praise and worship for God the Father, God the Son, and God the Holy Spirit for all eternity. But Lucifer developed a pride problem. He wanted to be lifted up. He wanted to be higher than the throne of God, and his pride led to his destruction.

The prophet Isaiah tells us that Lucifer fell from heaven, and he became known as Satan:

> How have you fallen from heaven, O light-bringer and daystar, son of the morning! How you have been cut down to the ground, you who weakened and laid low the nations [O blasphemous, satanic king of Babylon!] And you said in your heart, I will ascend to heaven; I will exalt my throne above the stars of God; I will sit upon the mount of assembly in the uttermost north. I will ascend above the heights of the clouds; I will make myself like the Most High. Yet you shall be brought

down to Sheol (Hades), to the innermost recesses of the pit (the region of the dead). Those who see you will gaze at you and consider you, saying, Is this the man who made the earth tremble, who shook kingdoms?—Who made the world like a wilderness and overthrew its cities, who would not permit his prisoners to return home? All the kings of the nations, all of them lie sleeping in glorious array, each one in his own sepulcher. But you are cast away from your tomb like a loathed growth or premature birth or an abominable branch [of the family] and like the raiment of the slain; and you are clothed with the slain, those thrust through with the sword, who go down to the stones of the pit [into which carcasses are thrown], like a dead body trodden underfoot. You shall not be joined with them in burial, because you have destroyed your land and have slain your people. May the descendants of evildoers nevermore be named! Prepare a slaughtering place for his sons because of the guilt and iniquity of their fathers, so that they may not rise, possess the earth, and fill the face of the world with cities.

—ISAIAH 14:12–21, AMP

I think it's interesting that many of the fights in churches today begin in the music department. If you want to see people get really upset, start changing the music. Move the piano. Put a microphone by the drums. Give a solo to someone new. Ban the tambourine.

When my father-in-law became the pastor of a small church in Florida, there were many musical instruments in the church sanctuary. He told me that for one service, the worship team used five guitars, a piano, an organ, two or three tambourines, and a wash-tub bass fiddle—and each musician was vying to be the loudest. When my father-in-law decided to limit the number of musical instruments in the small church, there was an exodus of people who were greatly offended that he had the audacity to change their music.

Music is a powerful force. Many recording artists began their musical training in the church. Elvis Presley found his initial musical inspiration in an Assemblies of God church that he attended with his family.[1] The Oak Ridge Boys began as a Southern gospel group in the 1950s.[2] Whitney Houston began performing in the junior gospel choir at New Hope Baptist church in Newark, New Jersey. Her mother was also a gospel singer.[3] Little Richard's family was deeply religious, and he grew up as a part of AME, Baptist, and Pentecostal churches.[4] These people all became stars as a result of their early training in the church. They learned to sing from the heart and with the passion of a worshipper. The same heart can produce positive or negative emotion, depending on what influences the singer or musician.

Music can lead you into the very presence of God or into the depths of hell. Throughout history music has been used to steer culture and drive change. It is not the style of music that is the problem; musical styles of both Christian and secular music change with different generations, and those styles are not right or wrong. It is the heart behind it and the song lyrics that determine whether or not music brings glory to God. Music was created to glorify God. When we sing or play music that does not honor God, we betray Him.

Lucifer decided that he wanted to be above God, that he was more important than God. One-third of the angels followed him into the error of pride and self-exaltation, and all of heaven went to war. Satan lost and was cast out of heaven with the fallen angels who became the demons, principalities and powers, and rulers of darkness the Bible talks about in Ephesians

6. They lifted themselves against God and manifested betrayal. Before that time there had been no sin. Lucifer fell due to his pride. Pride led to sin, and sin led to betrayal. Had Lucifer never become prideful, there would have never been sin, and sin would have never brought betrayal into heaven.

Betrayal in the Garden

The next time we see betrayal in Scripture is in the Garden of Eden. In Genesis 2:25 the Bible says that Adam and Eve walked with God, and they were naked and not ashamed. They were not ashamed because they were not aware of sin. God created them without a sin nature, but He gave them free, moral choice. In other words, their actions were made of their own choice and no one else's. Ours are as well. We must take responsibility for the things we do. Adam and Eve had the ability to choose to obey or reject God's mandates and with that choice came the responsibility to face the consequences of their actions. God told Adam in Genesis 2:17 that the consequences of disobedience would be death.

The angels also had the ability to choose whether to serve God or reject Him. One-third of the angels chose to follow Lucifer, or Satan. We do not know how they were deceived into breaking allegiance to God, but we know they did.

> And war broke out in heaven: Michael and his angels fought with the dragon; and the dragon and his angels fought, but they did not prevail, nor was a place found for them in heaven any longer. So the great dragon was cast out, that serpent of old, called the Devil and Satan,

who deceives the whole world; he was cast to the earth,
and his angels were cast out with him.

—REVELATION 12:7–9

Most people know the story of Adam and Eve in the Garden of Eden. Satan deceived them into eating of the forbidden fruit, and sin entered the world. Some would like to believe that Satan first tempted Eve with the forbidden fruit because she was weak-minded. That is not true. When Satan as the serpent came and deceived Eve, he knew that she had not walked with God as long as Adam had and that her relationship with God was, in many ways, an extension of Adam's.

God created Adam first and had spent more time with him; Adam had the maturity and understanding that time brings to a relationship. Adam knew the consequence of disobedience was death. If Satan had gone to Adam and asked him, "Did God really say...," Adam probably would have said, "Yes, God did say..." God had told Adam that he was not to eat from the tree of the knowledge of good and evil. Adam had received this message firsthand. God had not told Eve this; it was Adam's responsibility to relay the information to her.

Because it is so clear that Adam knew exactly what God desired and expected of him, we can trace the betrayal in the garden to him. It boils down to this: Adam chose Eve over God, his Father. Adam rejected God to satisfy the desires of his wife. God had experienced betrayal in heaven with Lucifer and one-third of the angels. Then He created mankind and again faced betrayal. Due to his betrayal, Satan lost his position as one of the three archangels and was cast out of heaven. Due to their betrayal, Adam and Eve lost their status as friends of God and were cast out of the Garden of Eden. They had been living in a perfect world; there was no work, no toil, no arguing, no bloodshed between people or animals; the lion was lying next to the lamb. Suddenly all of the peace was shattered. In one moment sin entered the world.

As God told Adam, there are consequences for sinning against Him, and there are consequences for betrayal. When sin entered into the world, Adam and Eve realized they were naked and that they could no longer walk with the Creator. God cursed all three of those who were involved in the betrayal: the serpent, the man, and the woman. The serpent would have to crawl on its belly, and there would be enmity (hostility, hatred, ill will, animosity, and antagonism) between it and the woman. Eve would have pain in childbirth, and Adam would have to toil for food. The ground would no longer freely produce for him, but he would live by the sweat of his brow.

God pronounced these curses and their effect is still felt today. The serpent still crawls on the ground and there is hatred between it and womankind. There is still pain in childbirth despite medical advances, and mankind is still toiling to make a living in this world.

In Genesis 3:22–23 God sent Adam and Eve out of the Garden of Eden. In the garden was not only the tree of the knowledge of good and evil but also the tree of life. Had Adam and Eve remained in the garden, they would have been able to choose to live forever. Remember, they had free, moral choice. At any time they could have reached out and partaken of the fruit of the tree of life. God did not want that for mankind. He wanted redemption and the death of all sinfulness. To begin this process, He had to banish Adam and Eve from the garden:

> Then the LORD God said, "Behold, the man has become like one of Us, to know good and evil. And now, lest he put out his hand and take also of the tree of life, and eat, and live forever"—therefore the LORD God sent

him out of the garden of Eden to till the ground from which he was taken. So He drove out the man; and He placed cherubim at the east of the garden of Eden, and a flaming sword which turned every way, to guard the way to the tree of life.

—GENESIS 3:22–24

God did not design the human body to die but to live forever. In God's love and grace He put man outside of Eden, and He put an angel at the entrance of the garden to prevent man's reentry. He judged mankind at that time. He judged man so that he could find grace. How could this be grace? If fallen man had partaken of the tree of life, he would have lived eternally in his sinfulness. But God had an alternate plan: He would provide a perfect sacrifice, and the seed of the woman would bruise the serpent's head.

And I will put enmity between you and the woman, and between your seed and her Seed; He shall bruise your head, and you shall bruise His heel.

—GENESIS 3:15

God prophetically declared the coming of a Savior and Redeemer, the Lord Jesus Christ!

The Third Betrayal

There was betrayal in heaven, betrayal in the garden, and then more betrayal in Adam and Eve's family. The first betrayal was about who God was. The second betrayal was about who would be God. The third betrayal was about how God would be worshipped.

This third betrayal is found in Genesis 4. Cain and Abel

brought offerings to the Lord. Cain, a tiller of the ground, brought the fruits of his labors. Abel, a keeper of the flocks, brought fat portions from his flock. Abel offered a sacrifice, an atonement for sin. Cain's offering, on the other hand, did not require anything to die. Cain presumed God would accept his offering; he presumed that *his* way to worship God would be acceptable. At the root of this betrayal was whom Cain would put in charge of his life. Would He accept God's dictates or live by his own?

> By faith Abel offered to God a more excellent sacrifice than Cain, through which he obtained witness that he was righteous, God testifying of his gifts; and through it he being dead still speaks.
> —HEBREWS 11:4

When Cain saw that God did not accept his sacrifice, he began to sulk. God noticed and warned Cain that sin was getting ready to enter into his heart and life. Cain's anger was a doorway for sin because sin begins in the heart. Although the sin Cain would commit against his brother had already begun in his heart, Cain still had a choice; he did not have to act on his desires. He could have stopped his sulking and sought forgiveness. Instead Cain did not heed God's voice and murdered his brother Abel.

With this betrayal, there again was a consequence. God marked Cain as a murderer and cursed him. God sent Cain away from the family to be a fugitive and a vagabond. Cain's betrayal kept him from having fellowship with his family. By killing his brother, he had betrayed his entire family.

> And He said, "What have you done? The voice of your brother's blood cries out to Me from the ground. So now you are cursed from the earth, which has opened its mouth to receive your brother's blood from your hand.

When you till the ground, it shall no longer yield its strength to you. A fugitive and a vagabond you shall be on the earth."

And Cain said to the Lord, "My punishment is greater than I can bear! Surely You have driven me out this day from the face of the ground; I shall be hidden from Your face; I shall be a fugitive and a vagabond on the earth, and it will happen that anyone who finds me will kill me."

And the Lord said to him, "Therefore, whoever kills Cain, vengeance shall be taken on him sevenfold." And the Lord set a mark on Cain, lest anyone finding him should kill him.

—Genesis 4:10–15

In the Gospel of Matthew Jesus recounted what He saw in Cain's life before Cain killed his brother:

You have heard that it was said to those of old, "You shall not murder, and whoever murders will be in danger of the judgment." But I say to you that whoever is angry with his brother without a cause shall be in danger of the judgment. And whoever says to his brother, "Raca!" shall be in danger of the council. But whoever says, "You fool!" shall be in danger of hell fire. Therefore if you bring your gift to the altar, and there remember that your brother has something against you, leave your gift there before the altar, and go your way. First be reconciled to your brother, and then come and offer your gift. Agree with your adversary quickly, while you are on the way with him, lest your adversary deliver you to the judge, the judge hand you over to the officer, and you be thrown

into prison. Assuredly, I say to you, you will by no means
get out of there till you have paid the last penny.

—MATTHEW 5:21–26

Notice first of all that Abel brought a sacrifice, a spotless
lamb, and laid it before the Lord. Cain saw that Abel's offering
was accepted and that God's favor and anointing were on Abel.
He saw the anointing and became angry. Cain then brought his
own offering to the Lord. It was not his first fruits or his best,
and God did not accept it. God wanted the first fruits, the best of
what Cain had to offer, not the leftover, last-minute, last thought.
God knew when Cain walked up to that altar that his heart was
not right. He was angry with his brother without a cause. Abel
had done nothing to harm him. Abel had only worshipped God
the way he was supposed to. Instead of leaving his gift at the altar
and going to make things right with his brother, Cain continued
with the sacrifice. God rejected the sacrifice because it was not
given with a clean, pure heart.

When we come to the altar we are to come with the right
offering and the right heart. When we do this, we will be
accepted. God does not want us to begrudge our gifts to him.
God loved both Cain and Abel. He did not love one more than
the other but Abel gave an offering to God in the manner he was
supposed to give it.

We see in these examples from Scripture that betrayal is
rooted in pride. The act of betrayal always stems from someone
wanting to be exalted somehow, wanting to be in control, or
wanting to be worshipped. This is what can drive a spouse, a
brother, a parent, a close friend, or a mentor to betrayal. They
are more concerned about satisfying their own wants and desires
than honoring God, obeying Scripture, and respecting the relationships they once valued.

When our priorities and values go off course, we are all susceptible to betrayal. We are all vulnerable to inflicting hurt on others when we choose to make someone or something lord in our lives besides God. Knowing how easily mankind could fall prey to these temptations, God created signposts to help us know if we are going in the right direction. Those signposts are called the Ten Commandments. Understanding them will shed more light on our responsibilities to God.

Chapter 2

THE TEN COMMANDMENTS: GOD'S PROTECTION FROM BETRAYAL

Have you ever had an *aha* moment? You know, one of those times in your life when you said, "Why didn't I see that before?" That is what happened to me when I started looking at the Ten Commandments from God's point of view. God was the first to feel the devastation of betrayal, first in heaven and then again in the Garden of Eden. We know that God is loving and gracious, but He is also a God of order and justice.

Many think the Ten Commandments were given to bring order and establish a moral code. This is true, but I believe the Lord wanted to use the commandments for another purpose. Could the Ten Commandments have been given because God did not want us to experience the same devastation He felt in heaven and in the Garden of Eden? I think we can say yes to that possibility without violating any biblical understanding or purposes.

After coming to this realization, I began to look at the Ten

Commandments as not just a moral and civil law but also as an expression of God's compassion, mercy, and love being demonstrated to mankind. This was the first written document of God's love and grace to mankind. This is one of the reasons that Moses became so angry when he came down off Mount Sinai.

He had just received the greatest written gift of love and kindness in the history of the world, but when he came to deliver that message, the very people it was written for were dishonoring this great, loving God by worshipping a golden calf they had made. As the Lord was giving the Israelites a document that would protect them from betrayal, they were in the very act of betraying Him!

Signposts to Protect Us

You must understand that before God gave the people of Israel the Ten Commandments, He had established Himself as their God, the mighty One who brought them out of the land of sin and bondage. In giving them these new commandments, He was promising not just to deliver them but, as their God, to also keep them from slavery. With this promise there was an unspoken understanding: follow Me with your whole heart and walk in freedom, or forsake Me and walk back into sin and bondage.

How the Israelites chose to respond to God's commandments would determine the quality of their future. As we look at these commandments, let's consider how God sees them and what they can show us about betrayal.

1. You shall have no other gods before Me.

> And God spoke all these words, saying: "I am the LORD your God, who brought you out of the land of Egypt, out

of the house of bondage. You shall have no other gods before Me."

—Exodus 20:1–3

God wanted nothing between us and Him, nothing that would draw our attention away from the love He has for us. In this first commandment He was saying, "Don't betray Me by worshipping another god. Be loyal to Me." We worship what we love. We often hear people say, "I love that shop. I love that food. I love going there. I love that sport. I love going to the gym. I love my new car. I love my children. I love my spouse." While there is nothing wrong with enjoying the things and people God puts in our lives, there comes a time when we have to differentiate between what we really love and what we worship.

Worship is based on trust and relationship. When the Lord said, "Thou shalt have no other gods before me," He was protecting us. Other gods lie, deceive, and manipulate. Our God is the opposite. Throughout Scripture the Lord tells us that He does not change, He cannot lie, and He will never forsake us. Each of these statements is powerful in its own right but collectively they show God to be someone who can be trusted, someone in whom we can have faith.

Through the first commandment the Lord was telling us not to put anything above Him because He's the only God who will never betray us! Again and again God promises us a relationship that He will never betray (Deut. 31:6, 8; Josh. 1:5; Matt. 28:20; Heb. 13:5–6). Do you see how important this is?

The most important relationship in our lives is with God. It is a relationship that has eternal significance, and God wants it to be based on trust. As someone who has felt the sting of betrayal in several areas of my life, I can testify to the fact that it was the security that I felt in the presence of God that drew me to Him and has kept me close to Him during my Christian walk. I have never heard the words "I don't love you" from the Lord. Never in my quiet time with God have I ever heard or sensed those words! I have heard, "You have disappointed Me; repent." Or, "I can't bless you if you do that." But never have I heard, "I don't love you." That is why I can forgive others when I am betrayed—because I have a secure relationship with Jesus Christ that is based on trust and love. This relationship of trust and love allows me to trust and love others.

Jesus wanted to be one with the Father (John 10:30) and to do the Father's will (John 6:38). He did not want to betray His relationship with His heavenly Father. That is why Jesus's cry on the cross was so significant. When He said, "My God, My God, why have You forsaken Me?" (Matt. 27:46), He was acknowledging a severance in His relationship with the Father.

When the sins of all mankind, past, present, and future, were laid on Jesus's shoulders, God turned His face from Jesus, because to God sin is the greatest betrayal in the world. The Father and the Son had enjoyed unbroken fellowship until that moment in time, and it was sin that broke the relationship. Because Jesus suffered that separation from the Father, you and I never have to experience that. Hallelujah! Putting God first is a way of protecting yourself from the sting of betrayal.

2. You shall not make for yourself a carved image.

> You shall not make for yourself a carved image—any likeness of anything that is in heaven above, or that is in the earth beneath, or that is in the water under the earth; you shall not bow down to them nor serve them. For I, the LORD your God, am a jealous God, visiting the iniquity of the fathers upon the children to the third and

fourth generations of those who hate Me, but showing mercy to thousands, to those who love Me and keep My commandments.

—Exodus 20:4–6

Mankind constantly looks for something to worship, but we are not to worship anything other than God. The first commandment is that we put nothing above our love for God. The second is similar in that we are not to make any kind of image and bow down to it. One commandment deals with the heart, the other deals with both our hearts and our actions.

Idols, statues, pictures, charms, and amulets can carry demonic supernatural power, but we are to seek power only from God. We are to esteem only Him. We are commanded not to worship trees, animals, people, money, mother earth, our bodies, angels, movie stars, music personalities, any other person or thing God has created.

No created thing can adequately depict God or His holiness. His Word tells us:

You saw no form of any kind the day the LORD spoke to you at Horeb out of the fire. Therefore watch yourselves very carefully, so that you do not become corrupt and make for yourselves an idol, an image of any shape, whether formed like a man or a woman, or like any animal on earth or any bird that flies in the air, or like any creature that moves along the ground or any fish in the waters below. And when you look up to the sky and see the sun, the moon and the stars—all the heavenly array—do not be enticed into bowing down to them and worshiping things the LORD your God has apportioned to all the nations under heaven.

—Deuteronomy 4:15–19, NIV

Every one of us is created to worship, but that worship is to be directed only toward God Almighty, the Alpha and the Omega, the beginning and the end. You cannot count on money or mother earth or people to never let you down. But God can always be trusted.

3. You shall not take the name of the Lord in vain.

> You shall not take the name of the LORD your God in vain, for the LORD will not hold him guiltless who takes His name in vain.
>
> —EXODUS 20:7

God commands us not to take His name in vain. He is basically saying, "Don't betray Me and My holiness with vulgarity." God gave this commandment so we would understand the value of His name. We are to respect His name just as we respect Him by not putting anything above Him. When I hear good things about people I do not know, it often makes me want to meet those individuals. In the same way, whenever I hear something bad about someone, I am on my guard when I'm around them. Our words affect others' perspectives.

We have all been around people who, in trying to be funny, have said negative things about their spouses. Two things usually happen in these cases: first, the spouse feels betrayed by the reckless comment (especially if the spouse is the opposite of the way he or she was described); second, smart people decide that they do not want to be in a close relationship with someone who would speak so carelessly about his or her spouse. Esteeming God enough to not use His name carelessly or without purpose is one way we honor Him and make others aware that He is someone who is worth knowing because He is worthy of our respect.

4. Remember the Sabbath day, to keep it holy.

> Remember the Sabbath day, to keep it holy. Six days you
> shall labor and do all your work, but the seventh day is
> the Sabbath of the LORD your God. In it you shall do
> no work: you, nor your son, nor your daughter, nor your
> male servant, nor your female servant, nor your cattle,
> nor your stranger who is within your gates. For in six
> days the LORD made the heavens and the earth, the
> sea, and all that is in them, and rested the seventh day.
> Therefore the LORD blessed the Sabbath day and hal-
> lowed it.
>
> —EXODUS 20:8–11

God is saying, "Don't betray My gifts by failing to recognize
them." The day of rest was designed by God for us to regain our
strength for the coming week. It is a gift for us to utilize! Can you
imagine being given a gift and never using that gift or abusing it?

I once had a friend who was a borderline hoarder. Whenever
he was given a gift, he would place it on a shelf in his closet
so he could use it someday. Through the years his gifts, often
consisting of shirts and sweaters, were boxed and stacked in his
closet. He had so many unused gifts that he lost track of what he
actually had. Many of those gifts became unusable as they went
out of style or dry rotted. "Someday" never came, but he did not
realize that his gifts were being wasted by his lack of use.

When a gift is given but never used, it conveys a message to
the recipient that it is not appreciated or that it is disliked. By
abusing or never using the gift of the Sabbath, we are telling the
giver that we do not honor the gift.

The Sabbath is also a time for us to reflect on the goodness
of God and how He has blessed us. Relationships have to be cul-
tivated or they will break down and betrayal will occur. I have

counseled hundreds of couples, and invariably I hear the same statement when a marriage is in crisis: "We never talk, and I do not feel like I am a priority anymore." Honoring the Sabbath is a mechanism that helps us honor our most important relationship! By taking care of our relationship with God and those most important to us, we can safeguard ourselves from betrayal.

5. Honor your father and mother.

> Honor your father and your mother, that your days may be long upon the land which the LORD your God is giving you.
>
> —EXODUS 20:12

Don't betray your parents with disrespect. When you betray them, you betray God. God has put them in your life as an authority. Even as an adult you are to honor your parents. You may not always agree with them, but you can disagree with your parents without being disrespectful. This does not mean that you allow your parents to control your life; it means that you listen to them and consider their suggestions. You may not utilize their advice, but it is good to hear them out.

I remember many things about my childhood. Some of those memories are funny while others are painful. I was given up for adoption as a baby and struggled with rejection for many years as a result. I developed ways of dealing with rejection that often were neither kind nor respectful. I had "hot buttons" that could be pushed if someone said something even remotely negative about my adoptive mother. I realize now that this was born out of my own insecurities, but I also know that even when I handled a situation badly, my reaction came from a sincere desire to love and respect my parents and their good name.

The Lord wants us to treat our parents with respect so that

we can model that esteem for our own children and thus not be betrayed by them in the later stages of life. I have been in ministry long enough to see a lot of things and grow in my understanding of people. One thing I have noticed is that the children who honor and respect their parents usually have very stable homes of their own and are close to their extended family.

I have watched men I revere become grandparents and even great-grandparents. Their children, grandchildren, and even great-grandchildren honor and respect them. When I ask them the secret to fostering that honor and respect, they always refer back to the times they spent doing fun things with their children. Among those fun times were attending family gatherings and keeping their children in healthy spiritual climates.

Each commandment builds on the previous one. Through them the Lord teaches us how to protect our primary relationships from betrayal. When we honor God, His presence, His holiness, His name, and His authority in our lives, we guard ourselves against the very thing that brought sin into heaven: betrayal.

6. You shall not murder.

> You shall not murder.
>
> —EXODUS 20:13

This commandment is not talking about pacifism. It is saying we must not betray the sanctity of life. We live in a nation where life is not valued as it once was. I have a hard time understanding politicians who want to ban gun ownership in America but will support abortion. There were roughly 1.21 million abortions in 2008, down from about 1.29 million in 2002, approximately 1.31 million in 2000, and 1.36 million in 1996. Abortion has been responsible for legally ending the lives of nearly 50 million babies in the United States alone since the *Roe v. Wade* decision in 1973.[1] Outside the United States there have been approximately 40 million abortions per year since 1980, which is more than 1.2 billion babies killed.[2]

By legalizing abortion, we violated this basic tenet of the sanctity of human life, and betrayal started to shape America's emotional landscape more and more. Since 2011, and for the first time in American history, there are more children in blended families or single-parent homes than in "traditional" homes with both biological parents present. We are just now seeing the real damage this has done to America.

We may never know all of the cultural effects abortion has brought us, but we can look at the economic effects of the betrayal of this commandment. America is just beginning to surface from the worst recession since the Great Depression. One wonders if it would ever have happened if those 42 million aborted babies had been born and produced children of their own. Conservative estimates say there would be at least 69 million more people living in America right now. That means we would have needed more homes, schools, colleges, hospitals, stores, clothes—you get the picture. This would have had a significant impact on our economy, but we lost out on this possibility because we decided to betray a God who was trying to protect us.

7. You shall not commit adultery.

> You shall not commit adultery.
>
> —EXODUS 20:14

Adultery is defined as voluntary sexual intercourse between a married person and someone other than his or her lawful spouse. An expanded definition is any sexual activity outside of marriage. This includes sex before marriage, pornography, lust, lewdness, or sexual misconduct. God does not want the marriage covenant betrayed. Adultery is a form of betrayal. If you betray a covenant on earth, you will betray your covenant with God.

In a recent survey 21 percent of men and nearly 15 percent of women admitted to infidelity.[3] That is staggering. Maybe that is why young adults are waiting longer and longer to get married. People in our culture right now do not seem to trust marriage. Young adults have too often seen a negative picture of marriage rather than the covenant relationship God desires. This type of betrayal will emotionally wound people like no other type of betrayal.

God designed marriage to be the consummation of a blood covenant between a husband and wife. He never intended for divorce to occur and made provision for it only because of the hardness of mankind's heart. The devastation of this type of betrayal affects the nuclear family as well as the extended family. Adultery can be brutal; however, Jesus is powerful enough to bring hope and healing to the recipient and even the initiator of the betrayal.

8. You shall not steal.

You shall not steal.

—Exodus 20:15

Everyone has a legitimate right to obtain and own property. God wants us to honor and respect that right. Don't betray your neighbors by taking something that does not belong to you. God wants us to be good stewards of what He gives us and to help others safeguard their possessions by following His commandment to not take what does not belong to us.

Theft has grown in our nation and our culture. How many of us have relatives we cannot trust because whenever they come to visit something is missing when they leave? Whenever you walk into a mall or any store, you know you are being filmed by a security camera. There are even signs informing you of that fact. Businesses have hidden cameras to cut down on employee theft, and they place security on their computer systems so information cannot be stolen. Homes have security systems. Banks employ armed guards.

Churches are not exempt. Donations and offerings are tallied under the watchful eye of guards and cameras. Parishioners are warned not to leave their valuables unattended. Even with all the measures taken to guard against theft, billions of dollars are lost every year to thieves.

Let me bring this commandment down to a very simplistic idea: theft is taking what does not belong to you or using something that belongs to someone else. If you drink someone's beverage in the break room refrigerator, you stole it, even if you intended to replace it. If you borrow something from someone's desk and never return it, you stole it. If you spend work time playing games on the office computer, you are stealing time from your employer. "Sharing" music recordings with friends is stealing if you make unsanctioned copies. When I was a child, a thief was one of the worst things you could be. Today many movies encourage theft by portraying it as a fun prank, thus destigmatizing the act.

People often do not trust one another because they have been betrayed through theft. When we first moved to the suburbs of Atlanta, my wife was so excited because every house we looked at had an alarm system that was up to date. We were coming from a community where you could leave your windows open at night and only latch the screen door. She told her friends how modern everything was. I did not have the heart to tell her at the time that the reason everything was so modern was because the crime rate was so high. This was in 1993, and things have only gotten worse. Your homeowner's insurance and other insurance costs have risen because of theft. God wants us to honor, not betray, our neighbors.

9. You shall not bear false witness.

You shall not bear false witness against your neighbor.
—Exodus 20:16

Don't betray your friends by lying to or about them. A person who lies or deceives does not have the spirit of God in him. Jesus said that He was the way, the truth, and the life (John 14:6). Truth was important to God from the very beginning of time and remains so today. Our justice system in America is based on truth. In a courtroom a person who is testifying places his hand on a Bible and promises to tell the truth, the whole truth, and nothing but the truth.

There are no little lies or big lies; there are no white lies. There is only the truth and the lies. There are different types of liars, but liars are still liars. A pathological liar is someone who actually believes the lies he is telling. A protector liar convinces himself that it is actually better that the other person not know the real truth, because the truth would be too painful.

A compulsive liar is someone who lies because it has become a habit. He or she may also be a born liar, someone who will tell a lie even when the truth would be better. A habitual liar will lie about unimportant things. There are also deceiver liars, those who don't tell the entire story or keep certain facts hidden. This is often done to present the liar in a better light or to make a better story. If it is not the whole truth, it is a lie.

I was once in a meeting where a "friend" of mine bore false witness against me. He did it in a teasing manner, but he distorted the truth so that he could slam an organization with which I am involved. He told the story so well that he had me believing it until I went back and checked my records. I am now wondering how I can trust him again because of his actions. I have heard him "share" his feelings on other matters, and now I wonder how valid they were. Integrity is hard to earn but easily lost.

When Mark* first came to our church, he seemed to be a simple young man. After he attended for a few weeks, he requested a meeting with me and my administrator to discuss some financial issues. We met with him, and he proceeded to tell us that he had recently inherited $10 million from a neighbor who had thought of him as his own son. He wanted to pay his tithes to our church and to get some investment counseling. We brought in a CPA and an investment counselor to help him on his way. As time went on, we began to realize that his stories were not adding up. His car was frequently broken down. He was frequently short on cash and borrowing twenty dollars from various people in the church.

We decided to request a meeting with his wife, who was mortified that he had lied to another pastor. Not only had he not inherited any money, but he was also unwilling to work and provide for his own family. He had made his rounds through various churches, telling lies to make himself appear important. The truth was that he and his family were destitute, in need of a huge hand-up and some groceries. While this is an extreme example, it demonstrates that there are people who will lie and deceive for

_____

* Not his real name.

no apparent reason. This is betrayal. Your words and your deeds should match up every day!

10. You shall not covet.

> You shall not covet your neighbor's house; you shall not covet your neighbor's wife, nor his male servant, nor his female servant, nor his ox, nor his donkey, nor anything that is your neighbor's.
>
> —Exodus 20:17

Covetousness is an extreme desire to obtain another person's possessions. It can be a form of extreme greed or an insatiable desire to acquire wealth. In this commandment God is telling us that we are not to want what belongs to someone else. In the eighth commandment God said that we are not to take what belongs to someone else but in the tenth commandment He told us that we are not to even want it.

Do not betray the provision of the Lord. When we covet what someone else has, we are telling God that He is not big enough to supply our needs. That is why the Lord teaches His people to tithe and give offerings. When your focus is on God's goodness to you, you won't have a mind-set to covet. Every time I write a tithe check or give offerings, I am reminded of how good God has been to my family. Everything we have has been given to us by God. Therefore, He has access to everything that we have.

Jesus said we cannot serve God and mammon, which is the love of money and the worship of things:

> No one can serve two masters; for either he will hate the one and love the other, or else he will be loyal to the one and despise the other. You cannot serve God and mammon.
>
> —Matthew 6:24

Paul said that the love of money is the root of all evil:

> For the love of money is a root of all kinds of evil, for which some have strayed from the faith in their greediness, and pierced themselves through with many sorrows.
> —1 TIMOTHY 6:10

Again God uses one of His commands to gently and lovingly keep us from the potential of betrayal. When we covet, we are saying that we are discontent with our lot in life. God wants us to trust Him to always provide what we need, even if what we need is different from what God gives someone else.

The Ten Commandments are the greatest laws ever written. Through them God tells us: do not betray God, your friends, your neighbors, or your spouse. We do not have to worry about betraying God, our friends, neighbors, or spouse if we walk closely with God. When you walk closely with God, you are walking in His shadow, a dim replica of what we need to be. There is no better place to be than in the shadow of God.

Betrayal Is Not Failure

Perhaps you are thinking of some way in which you have been betrayed. In reality it may have been a failure. It is crucial to understand that there is a difference. To betray someone means to deliver them into the hands of an enemy by treachery or fraud. It also means to be unfaithful and to violate a trust. Betrayal is intentional. Failure is not.

During the Last Supper, Jesus told Peter and His other disciples that He was going to the cross and that some of them would flee from Him. Peter adamantly said that he would never forsake Jesus. Everyone else might do so, but he would not. Jesus then told Peter that Satan was going to sift Peter like wheat but that He (Jesus) was going to pray for his faith. Jesus then told Peter that he would deny Him three times before the night was over.

Peter failed the Lord, but it was never his intention to do so. It was the weakness of his flesh that kept him from standing tall in the face of opposition. Peter warmed himself by the fire as Jesus was beaten and tortured. Peter then denied Jesus three times. He failed Jesus, but he did not betray Him.

Judas, on the other hand, betrayed the Lord. It was deliberate, premeditated, and planned. It was carefully thought out. What Judas did was betrayal.

The difference between failure and betrayal is the premeditation and the intentionality of the act. We have all said and done things we wish we had never said or done. We have failed. Some of us view people in our lives as Judases when, in reality, they have simply failed us. They have caused us disappointment. They have hurt us in a particular moment. This is what happened with Peter. He said and did something in a moment of time that he greatly regretted. Even though he made the mistake three times and not just once, his actions were never premeditated or intentional; Peter failed Jesus, but he didn't betray Him.

Why Betrayal Hurts So Much

When Jesus was in the Garden of Gethsemane, He was praying and began to sweat great drops of blood. This is an actual medical condition called *hematidrosis*, which is caused by great levels of psychological stress and fear. As the body produces sweat, the extreme stress and fear causes that sweat to literally become bloody. This causes the skin to be very fragile and sensitive. A simple touch to the head would have been excruciating.[4]

Already in physical and spiritual pain Jesus stood as Judas appeared with a mob. Jesus asked, "Judas, is that you?" Judas walked toward Jesus and kissed Him. To the Western mind that is not significant; to the Eastern mind, it is very significant. You only kiss someone with whom you are in covenant. To betray a covenant is unthinkable. When Judas betrayed Jesus, he betrayed a covenant. He produced in Jesus not just physical pain but also the spiritual and emotional pain that accompanies the betrayal.

We will look at some characteristics of betrayers in later chapters, but for now I want to point out a common thread that explains why betrayal hurts so much. *Only those close to you can betray you.* Jesus warned Judas several times about the betrayal that was in his heart. Jesus knew it was there before Judas ever came to the point of planning and executing his plan.

When you have a Judas in your life, he will be a part of your inner circle. He will have walked with you on a personal, intimate level. Although I did not know it at the time, my first Judas experience was with my birth parents; the very ones who should have loved and cared for me rejected me before I was ever born. Your Judas may have been a partner in business, a member of your board, a confidante, a best friend, a spouse, a child, a close family member, or a parent.

Whatever role they play in your life, more than likely you thought you could put your life in their hands and be safe. In your wildest imagination you would not have thought this person capable of betraying you. No matter how painful the betrayal, you can rest assured that God knows how you feel. He felt the sting of betrayal not only in heaven, in the Garden of Eden, and again in the Garden of Gethsemane, but He also feels it when we refuse to turn away from sin.

In John 6, after Jesus had chosen all of His disciples, He

said, "Did I not choose you, the twelve, and one of you is a devil?" (v. 70). He was referring to Judas, knowing he would betray Him. Jesus was not extending judgment toward Judas; He was extending grace. This may seem like an awkward thing for Jesus to say, but what He was doing was really profound. He was giving Judas the opportunity to walk toward grace and repent, but Judas refused the grace offered to him and continued on his road to destruction.

Just as Jesus recognized and exposed Judas's betrayal, He recognizes and exposes our betrayal. We often take great offense to that, but we need to learn that it is not God's judgment but His grace that exposes our sin. God is rich in mercy. He doesn't want any of His children to suffer. That is why He gave us the Ten Commandments and why He warns us when we are going off track—because He loves us.

Chapter 3

GUARD YOUR HEART

I WAS BORN ON June 8, 1960, and three days later was given up for adoption. Throughout my life I was told that I was of Italian ancestry, and I thought that I was probably born because two teenagers did not use birth control. I never really thought I needed to know about my birth parents or the circumstances of my birth. It was only after my oldest daughter became very unexplainably ill that I considered trying to trace my genetic history.

My wife and I gathered the information I had been given, and we started searching for my genetic roots. Although I had been told that my adoption records were unsealed, that was not the case. We tried various ways to get more information but made no progress. We registered on websites and databases to no avail. According to the state of New York, my records were sealed and could never be opened except by a court order. The court order could only be obtained as a matter of life or death. We were at an impasse and did not know which way to turn.

As my daughter's physical condition became worse, we became more desperate and hired a private firm to handle the search. Within a short time we had most of the answers we sought…and some of the answers I did not want to hear.

I learned that my birth mother and father were having an affair when I was conceived. Both were married to other people and worked at the same hospital in upstate New York. She was a medical secretary, and he was an Iranian surgeon. The affair had been ongoing for quite some time, and I was not the first pregnancy. Each time she conceived, he would perform an illegal abortion on her. Not only had they betrayed their own spouses, but they had also betrayed all of the babies they conceived together—and they ultimately betrayed me.

In the fall of 1959 my birth father was asked to return to Iran and perform a surgical procedure on a high-ranking government official. He left immediately and returned the following spring, not knowing that my birth mother was pregnant and too far advanced for him to perform an abortion on her.

My birth mother was forced to carry me full term, knowing that she would give me up for adoption. She and her husband had reconciled, and one of her greatest fears was that I would look too different from her other four children. At the hospital she asked the nursing staff to cover my face with a blanket so she would not see me. She felt that if she ever saw my face she would not be able to give me up. They did as she asked, and it was the year 2000 before she ever saw my face.

Research seems to show that a baby can sense a mother's rejection while still in the womb. I cannot say that is always the case, but I do know that although I was shown great love and support in my early life, I always felt like I was not good enough or that I didn't measure up. I felt that I had somehow failed and that there was some grave reason my birth family didn't want me. I wondered (hoped even) if they had been too poor to keep me. Poverty would have given me a way to explain why I was given up for adoption.

My adoptive parents were a French man named Norman who fell in love with a second-generation Russian/Polish woman who had a call of God on her life. June, my mother, had been in Bible school, training to be a missionary, when she became ill and had to return home. Doctors found that she had problems with her kidneys and would never be able to fulfill her dream of being a missionary.

When she returned to Bible school, the young man she was planning to marry had found someone else. Brokenhearted, she went back home where she met, fell in love, and eventually married Norman. Due to her inability to have children, she told God that if He would give her children, she would give them back to Him. It was a true Hannah prayer. (See 1 Samuel 1:25–27.)

After years of marriage June and Norman became the potential adoptive parents of a beautiful baby girl. They held her in their arms; then returned home to wait the required week before she would be released to go home with them. During that week, the birth mother decided that she wanted her child to go to someone else. June and Norman returned to the hospital to pick up their baby only to find that she was no longer theirs.

Brokenhearted, they sought the help of a local lawyer who put them on his list of families waiting to adopt. Due to the trauma they had just endured, the lawyer decided that the next available child, a girl, would be theirs. To everyone's surprise, my birth mother went into early labor and delivered me before the girl was born. True to his word, the attorney gave me, the next available child, to June and Norman. Shortly after I was adopted, my mother unexpectedly became pregnant, and the next spring she delivered a healthy baby boy. Eleven months separated me and my younger brother.

For as long as I can remember, I knew I was adopted. My parents chose to tell me as much as they knew about my birth. They wanted to assure me that they had "chosen" me and that I was loved. In 1960 there was a certain stigma associated with adoption, and I felt the sting of not being blood-related to my family.

I was "chosen" by parents who were never supposed to have biological children but then eventually did have their own child. In my mind I was not loved as much as my brother. I could not understand how anyone could love a person who was not related by blood, so I did not think they could possibly love me as much as they loved my brother, who was their "real" son. Whether real or imagined, I began to feel the sting of rejection.

I was one year ahead of my brother in school, and when he started school, I became known as his illegitimate brother. This only worsened the rejection that was beginning to take root in my life. I had no idea that being unwanted by my birth parents also contributed to those feelings.

The rejection that grew in me bore fruit of unresolved anger. I would get so angry I would explode, and I seemed to need to solve my problems with physical violence. I got into a fight almost every day of the school year, from elementary school through high school. Team sports became an outlet for my anger, but I still wasn't dealing with the real issue: rejection.

My mother conceived again when I was twelve years old and gave birth to my younger brother. During his birth, the doctors discovered that my mother had carried him in a womb that was filled with cancer. We did not know if either she or he would live long enough to come home from the hospital. God performed a miracle of healing on my mother and she did come home, bringing a tiny baby boy with her.

It was only as I held my baby brother in my arms for the first time that I finally understood how a person can love something or someone who is not blood-related to him. I loved him more than I could have imagined or understood. During the next few years, God used my brother Ray to help me understand the true meaning of love and acceptance. Ray went everywhere I went, did everything I did, and became a source of comfort to my wounded spirit. It did not matter to Ray that I was not his blood; I was his brother, and he loved me.

Although I had started the journey of healing, I still had not dealt with the deep-seated feelings of anger and rejection. They followed me into college and into many personal relationships. If there was ever a hint of rejection, I immediately responded with anger and often got into physical altercations.

During the time I was searching for my birth family, my wife, Jelly, assured me that my birth mother had never forgotten me, that she would always remember the baby she gave away. I will never forget the first time I spoke with my birth mother on the telephone and told her who I was.

She tearfully exclaimed, "I have been waiting on your call!"

We spoke for a few moments, then she asked me, "What color are you?"

Needless to say, I was taken aback and did not know how to respond. I had always thought I was white, possibly of Italian ancestry, but it seems that my birth father was a very dark Iranian man. Once again I felt the sting of rejection and betrayal. This time it was not because I was illegitimate, but because my color was different. For the first time in my life I felt prejudice.

I would love to tell you that my birth family was reunited,

and we all lived happily ever after, but that would not be true. But I did find my medical history and genetic roots, my birth parents, and four of my biological siblings, two of whom I am very much alike. I was able to be assured that my birth mother had a relationship with Jesus Christ before she died. I met my birth father, who is Muslim, and was able to share Christ and a Farsi Bible with him. To my knowledge he has never made a profession of faith, but I am still praying. His family knows nothing of me or my birth mother.

Beware of Bitterness

The feelings of rejection and betrayal that I had as a child and even as an adult are not that unique, but for many years I did not know what to do with them. Many who have faced betrayal will deal with emotions that can affect them for the rest of their lives if not addressed.

As a pastor I have had the opportunity to see the effects of betrayal in an up-close and very personal manner. A few years ago a young couple came into my office when she learned her husband was involved in an emotional affair with her best friend who was also married. These two couples were very close, vacationing together, trading off child care, and sometimes working together.

While she and her best friend were on a trip together, the betrayed woman noticed that every time her friend received a telephone call she stepped away from the group. She later found out that the private call her friend received was from the betrayed woman's husband. She was devastated to learn that her own husband, who had been too busy with work to spend much time on the phone with her, was spending hours talking on the telephone with her friend.

Both couples went to counseling and worked through the emotional infidelity, but the process was painful. Although they did not spend as much time together, the two women eventually resumed their friendship. The woman who had been betrayed tried to help the friend and hold her accountable for her conversation, attire, and actions. There was still not a high level of trust, but they were working to rebuild that too.

Two years after the initial betrayal, the best friend was involved in an affair with the husband of another friend. This time two marriages were destroyed. Although one of these couples tried very hard to rebuild their relationship, the other couple did not put as much effort into the process. The woman who had the history of infidelity did not successfully deal with the issues that led her to be unfaithful. She seemed to think everyone should forgive her and resume their relationships with her, regardless of her history and without her rebuilding trust or being held accountable. She wanted grace but no responsibility.

In her early years she had been betrayed by someone who should have loved and protected her but instead walked out of her life. Consistency and faithfulness were not demonstrated to her, and unfaithfulness became the norm for her life as well. She did not deal with the betrayal she experienced and never learned what to do with the pain she carried in her heart. As a result, she became a betrayer herself. She became the very thing she hated.

She did not delve into the deep parts of her soul and investigate why she repeatedly destroyed the lives and marriages of her friends and acquaintances. She never addressed the effect betrayal had on her emotional health and, even now, her actions continue to affect her life and the lives of those around her. This does not mean there is no hope for her; it simply means she must see the problem, address it, seek forgiveness, and work toward emotional and spiritual health.

One of the most prevalent emotions we must be aware of and guard against after experiencing betrayal is unforgiveness. Being unforgiving is deadly. If bitterness takes root in your heart, it will bear dangerous fruit that will affect other relationships.

The first aid protocol for wound care is to deal with it quickly: clean it, put ointment on it, and bandage it so it can heal. If a wound does not heal, it can spread infection throughout the body. People have had to get their limbs lanced or even amputated because a wound went untreated and infection set in. Forgiving the person or people who wronged you is the only way to heal from the wounds of betrayal and reclaim your joy.

When you are betrayed, the person who caused you pain tends to circulate in your mind. If you're unsure whom you may need to forgive, that is the person. You do not forgive for their sake but for yours. You are the one who is being hurt. You are the one who is carrying the wound with you wherever you go. You are the one who will not be able to face the future that God has planned for you.

Someone once said, "Forgiveness means that it is finally unimportant for you to hit back." When you reach that point, you will know that you have truly forgiven. You know you have truly forgiven when you no longer want to see the person who wronged you "get what's coming to them." You are able to sincerely pray that God blesses them.

There are times when we think we have addressed the wounds from a betrayal and have healed, but we don't realize there are still lingering problems. A few years ago Jelly was cleaning the back porch and got a splinter in her hand. She immediately removed the splinter and cleaned the wound, but because the splinter was impacted she ultimately had to get emergency care.

The wound was properly treated, but within less than twenty-four hours she was in the hospital with blood poisoning that required emergency surgery. We were warned that if she had not come to the hospital as quickly as she did, she could have died. She dealt with the wound quickly, she did what she was supposed to do, but this particular wound required more care.

In the same way we may think we are dealing with a wound quickly and adequately, not knowing that the anger and unforgiveness are still there. If we do not deal with our wounds thoroughly, our very spiritual, emotional, and mental lives could be in danger.

Bitterness Can Lead to Isolation

Many ministers of the gospel have been wounded by things that have happened in their ministries and because they never dealt with their pain, they cannot be nice to people. They put up a façade and go through life with a big wall around themselves, not letting anyone get close so they won't be hurt again. They let one situation destroy hundreds of potential healthy relationships.

In essence they become estranged. The word *estranged* means to be drawn apart from. Satan wants you to be estranged, or separated, from the love, power, and will of God.

No one wants to be wounded. No one likes being betrayed, but if we live long enough it will happen. It may cut you to the heart, but that does not mean that you stop loving people and doing what God has called you to do. You continue to love people because that is what Jesus did.

In John 21 Jesus was standing on the shore watching His

disciples. They had fished all night but had not caught anything. After Jesus told them to cast their nets onto the other side of the boat, the disciples caught so many fish that the nets began to break. Jesus then told them to bring over some of the fish and they would have breakfast. Jesus chose to have breakfast with Simon Peter *after* Peter had failed Him. He asked Peter, "Do you love Me?" The Amplified Bible says Jesus was asking Peter, "Do you love Me more than these [others do—with reasoning, intentional, spiritual devotion, as one loves the Father]?" (v. 15).

Peter replied, "You know that I love You [that I have deep, instinctive, personal affection for You, as for a close friend]" (v. 15, AMP). Jesus then told Peter to feed His lambs.

Jesus again asked Peter the same question and Peter replied the same way. Jesus then again told Peter to tend to His lambs.

When Jesus asked Peter the third time if he truly loved Him, Peter was hurt that Jesus would continue to ask the same question. Peter said to Jesus, "Lord, You know everything; You know that I love You [that I have a deep, instinctive, personal affection for You, as for a close friend]." To which Jesus replied, "Feed my sheep" (v. 17, AMP).

Many people do not understand the significance of this conversation between Jesus and Peter. Jesus wanted Peter to know that his job was not over, that he was still to "feed His sheep." Though Peter made a mistake, his calling had not changed. Jesus did not give up on Peter, and He doesn't want us to give up on others because we have been wounded.

The natural reaction to betrayal is to withdraw from everyone and close yourself off to relationships. That approach can make you unable or unwilling to find common ground and reach out with love and concern to others. This natural reaction can also cause bitterness to take root in your heart and begin to flourish.

As children we probably all picked dandelions and blew the soft flower heads away. What we did not know as children is that by blowing those "puff balls," we were actually blowing seeds all over the yard. Those seeds would find a place to land, take root, and begin to grow. They would then sprout more dandelions that would create seed, and the process would begin again. The unfortunate part of this is that dandelions can become a real nuisance to the yard man. Once they take root in a yard, they are quite difficult to eliminate.

Bitterness works exactly the same way. You may not know you are blowing seeds all over the place, but when those seeds take root they can become a great nuisance in our lives because they are almost impossible to eliminate. In the same way bitterness will grow and bear fruit, so be careful what you allow to take root in your heart. Bitterness is destructive.

Bitterness Hardens Your Heart

Just as hardened ground cannot receive seeds for planting, a hardened heart is not sensitive to the voice of God or the promptings of His Spirit. You have probably known people who never seem to smile. They are unhappy and always have a sour look on their faces. When you talk to them, there is frequently something wrong. Someone has treated them or a loved one badly, said something unkind, and made them angry. They are in a cycle of negativity. They have no joy and behave as if they have nothing to look forward to and nothing but dismal prospects.

These people have been wounded at some point and have become hardened in their spirits. They have no joy and no strength because they do not experience or take advantage of the presence of the Lord. They take one part of the Bible and apply it to themselves but leave out other parts of the Word. They serve God in certain areas but not in others. They become double-minded. They believe in God but often don't truly trust Him because of their wounds. This leads to a vicious cycle: because they doubt God, they cannot receive the miraculous in their lives. When miracles do not happen, they get mad at God or offended at His church. This will continue until defeat comes barreling into their lives.

The Bible is clear about the effects of double-mindedness:

> If any of you lacks wisdom, let him ask of God, who gives to all liberally and without reproach, and it will be given to him. But let him ask in faith, with no doubting, for he who doubts is like a wave of the sea driven and tossed by the wind. For let not that man suppose that he will receive anything from the Lord; he is a double-minded man, unstable in all his ways.
> —JAMES 1:5–8

I remember meeting a man like this when I was in my twenties. The man was a minister, which amplified the situation. He had a very negative attitude toward the ministry and toward life in general. The church where I was a pastor had grown from a few dozen to more than a hundred members. This person had a very well-established church with a large congregation. During a state meeting, I was sitting with a group of younger ministers. We were discussing our hopes and dreams for the future. This man walked up to us and interrupted our conversation. He began to berate us by saying that we really did not know what ministry was all about, and if we did we would get out while we could. He then began to tell us that many of us would not make it more than five years in full-time ministry because we were from a generation of quitters.

I do not know if he was having a bad day or if his bitterness surfaced just on that particular occasion. I remember thinking that I wanted to hear nothing he had to say. I walked away from that encounter a little discouraged but also bewildered that anyone would willingly attend this man's church. It was not long after that time that the attendance in his church began to dwindle. His attitude became apparent to the congregation. It had filtered into his conversation and his sermons. The church continued to lose members and eventually went from several hundred down to about twenty-five. It was at this point that the embittered minister retired.

Our paths again crossed about one year after he had retired. His attitude toward life in general was very bitter. The Holy Spirit reminded me of the verse in Songs of Solomon that says the little foxes spoil the vines (Song of Sol. 2:15). This simply means that little problems and issues, little "foxes," so to speak, can significantly damage a relationship when they are not addressed. Little foxes eat at the tender new growth of a vine and destroy the entire thing as a result. Little foxes do more damage than big foxes because they destroy new growth.

In retrospect, this man who had such a powerful ministry at one time had allowed bitterness to infiltrate his life and the little foxes, or problems, had spoiled his lifeline of ministry. No minister or leader can operate efficiently without a lifeline feeding the root system. That lifeline is the presence of God. Unfortunately, years earlier this minister had a confrontation with a board member that caused a major problem in the church. The anger and bitterness that resulted from the confrontation became a part of the minister's life. He was never able to let it go.

It is interesting to me that Satan did not immediately destroy the man through the bitterness but allowed a slow, deliberate death that damaged not only him and his emotional well-being but also those to whom he was supposed to minister. I often thought it would have been much better for that man and those around him if he had only dealt with his bitterness and anger immediately. This is one example of why it is so important for us to understand the effect bitterness can have on our lives.

I was once called to visit a woman who was sick and in the hospital. She did not attend our church, so I could visit her only after I had taken care of those in our congregation. As soon as I walked into the woman's hospital room she began to berate me for not coming sooner. I had sent a few other pastors, but she did not want them; she wanted me. Her first words to me were, "It's about time you got here." I ignored her jab at me and asked how she was doing. She began to tell me how sick she was and how bad the doctors, nurses, and dieticians were. She then started on her husband, who was sitting in the room with us. According to her, nothing in her life was good or had any value.

Hardened people have a difficult time receiving any help from God or His people because they are poisoned by their bitterness and cannot sense God's presence. As the apostle Paul wrote, they are "poisoned by bitterness and bound by iniquity" (Acts 8:23). The writer of Hebrews said:

> Pursue peace with all people, and holiness, without which no one will see the Lord: looking carefully lest anyone fall short of the grace of God; lest any root of bitterness springing up cause trouble, and by this many become defiled.
> —HEBREWS 12:14–15

The remedy for the poison of bitterness is to pursue holiness and to be at peace with everyone. This is hard for someone who has been hurt, but it is vital. When a heart is hard, the original feelings of hurt and rejection will turn into debilitating, crippling, life-draining, spirit-weakening anger. Unresolved anger will destroy whatever good qualities are left in your life. It will take over all of your relationships, your emotions, your spiritual life, and eventually your physical life.

It is no accident that the writer of Hebrews referred to bitterness as a root. The problem with roots is that they have the capacity to bear fruit of their own. People who have bitterness in their life toward a thing or individual will eventually see the same bitterness affect other areas. It does not just confine itself to the area it first affected. The root begins to spread.

Have you ever seen a root system of a large tree? When you observe the root system, you will see that there are primary and secondary roots that allow the tree to store food, be stable, and reproduce. Bitterness needs a root system in order to flourish. It receives sustenance and stability, and is able to reproduce by remaining in the life of the bitter person. When that root system is destroyed, the tree is destroyed because its life-giving sustenance is gone.

In the South we have a vine that has become a nuisance. It is called kudzu. It was introduced in 1876 to help prevent soil erosion. It worked too well. The leaf, the flower, and the root all have uses, including medicinal uses. The problem with using the root is that it is difficult to harvest. It can cover 150,000 acres annually if not held in check. Because it spreads so quickly, one way to keep it at bay is to dig it out of the ground. The root grows very deeply and in the red clay that is indigenous to our area, it is almost impossible to destroy. Just when you think it's gone, a little sprout will spring up and before you know it, you will have a nice crop of kudzu again covering your trees.

Bitterness is a lot like our kudzu. Once it takes root, it is difficult to get it out. Just when you think you have destroyed its root system, you will see a little sprout spring up. Then, before long, bitterness will cover every area of your life and destroy the things that give you life. Although kudzu has positive uses, it is often referred to as the "plant that ate the South." Bitterness has no use and can only be referred to as "the plant that eats hearts."

Bitterness Dulls Your Hearing

If bitterness takes root in a wounded person's life, he will not "hear" the Word. He will not hear the voice of God in the people the Lord sends to bring correction. Nor will they listen to encouragement. They will simply refuse to hear from anyone.

Occasionally someone will come to me and say he is not getting "fed" in our church. I once wondered how that was possible. I now understand that something can be wrong with a person's ability to receive from God. When people are being born again and filled with the baptism of the Holy Spirit in a church, something is wrong when someone says he or she cannot be fed.

When a person does not leave a church on good terms, he does not arrive at the next church on good terms. If he leaves offended, he will arrive offended, and he will not allow the Holy Spirit to minister to him.

Jelly uses this example: When you walk into the home of someone you plan to have dinner with, one of the first things you notice is the smell of food that is being prepared. Whatever foods you smell get you ready to partake of the dinner about to be served. However, if you walk into that same home with the same smells but are not feeling well, you do not have that same anticipation. You are not getting ready to be fed. You may even refuse certain items due to the fact that you are not well.

It is the same in our spiritual lives: when we walk into our Father's house, if we are unwell, we do not anticipate His presence or our time with Him. We may even refuse certain things due to the fact that we are unwell. It is all on the "table" for us to enjoy, but we choose to not do so.

I remember a situation that occurred in the life of a young pastor I have mentored. This young man moved to join the staff of a new church about two states away. At one point I led a conference with the leadership of this church, teaching them about relationships and honoring their pastor. The church began to grow and increased from four hundred to twelve hundred members within five years. Because of the growth, the congregation had to relocate and built a brand-new building.

Although God was really blessing this church, it had a history of problems. The congregation was constantly blaming the pastor for every little thing that occurred. My young mentee would call me frequently and ask my opinion on how to deal with a particular issue and then he would then go back into battle, trying to find resolution and peace for the body.

After a few years of difficulty he felt that God had released him from the church. The same day he felt the release from his place of ministry, I called him with a new ministry opportunity. He pursued the opportunity and after a time, decided that he and his family would make the move to another state to continue their ministry there.

A short while after my mentee decided to make the move, I began to receive e-mails from a man who was no longer in the church. Through a series of events this man became angry and bitter toward his pastor. He would not listen to anything his pastor had to say, either good or bad. He would not receive correction and was offended frequently. He was in the "house" but unable to be fed. His anger and bitterness eventually caused him to leave the church.

Although he left the church, he continued to act in anger and bitterness toward my mentee, trying to destroy both the man and the ministry. The man continued his vindictive behavior by sending the e-mails to me, the board at the new church, and anyone else who would listen. He said terrible things about his former pastor, trying to sabotage his new ministry post and keep the pastor from leaving. After a few of these e-mails I called this man and asked him, "If he is so bad, why do you want to keep him there?"

He responded by saying, "He just needs to stay here." Through conversation I realized that the man wanted his former pastor close so that he could continue to find ways to sabotage him. To me this seemed unbalanced and a ridiculous way to purse life, but his anger and bitterness had removed all of his capability to think clearly.

Bitter or Better?

If you carry offense around with you, it *will* bring bitterness and destruction into your life. Adrian Rogers was a great Baptist preacher from Memphis, Tennessee. About six months before he suddenly died, I had the privilege of meeting with him and four other pastors. It was one of the most wonderful times in my life. I spoke with him for a few minutes, asking him some questions related to leading a megachurch. In our conversation I told him that my pastor had once said that a pastor cannot build a great church without great heartache. Dr. Rogers put his head down and when he lifted it there was a tear in his eye.

He said, "You have a wise and godly pastor, don't you?"

I said, "Yes, sir."

"He is still your pastor, isn't he?"

I said, "Yes, sir, as a matter of fact, he is"

"You listen to him a lot, don't you?"

"Yes, sir."

Then Dr. Rogers said, "I can always tell someone who has a spiritual father because he treats authority differently and asks different kinds of questions."

I then asked him, "Sir, what is your great pain?"

He recounted this story[1]: "We had one car when our son was a baby. One day he got sick, and my wife called to tell me. I rushed home, and we quickly took him to the hospital. About halfway there my wife started screaming, 'I don't think he's breathing!' When we finally arrived at the hospital, the medical team did as much as they could, but my son died that day. My wife held our baby for one last time then we had to leave so the people from the funeral home could come to get him.

"We drove back to our parsonage, sat down at the table, and grabbed each other's hands. We looked at each other and said, 'We can get bitter or we can get better.'"

Dr. Rogers then opened his Bible and read from Job 1:

> Then Job arose, tore his robe, and shaved his head; and he fell to the ground and worshiped. And he said: "Naked I came from my mother's womb, and naked shall I return there. The LORD gave, and the LORD has taken away; blessed be the name of the LORD." In all this Job did not sin nor charge God with wrong.
>
> —Job 1:20–22

We are designed to trust God, trust family, trust leaders, and trust our nation. When we do not truly trust God, we cannot believe that He will see us through the darkness of betrayal or have confidence that He will again bring the miraculous into our lives. Without that foundation of trust, we will have no strength.

A *Reader's Digest* article titled "Why Do We Trust at All?" stated that people want to trust one another because it helps them to connect. It produces pleasurable feelings and helps to shape our culture. In other words, we need to be able to trust.[2]

Things will happen in life that we do not understand. During those times, we can choose to believe that though God gives and takes away, we can still trust Him. In the moments of our deepest betrayals, we can learn, as Job did, to not charge God with wrong.

Every loss requires us to walk through a process in order to recover. The pain of betrayal is real and personal. We cannot deny the pain. But if we acknowledge, accept, and treat the hurt and rejection we may feel, we will destroy the potential for bitterness to take root and flourish in our hearts.

Chapter 4

HOW TO IDENTIFY A BETRAYER

W
HEN OUR GRANDDAUGHTER was learning to walk, she decided she wanted to go up and down the stairs in our home. We put a barrier in front of the steps so she could not go up without our assistance. As she got older, she learned to climb around the barrier. One day it happened: she climbed up the steps without our help. She was so very proud of herself. She turned around and smiled, as if to say, "I knew I could do it!"

Although she had been shown time and again how to scoot down the steps on her bottom, she decided to walk back down her own way, not even holding on to the handrail. Before we could get to her, she fell head over heels all the way down. I thought my heart would break as she cried both from fear and from the pain of her fall. She was not hurt badly, but it was a long time before she tried to go up or down the steps without the assistance of her Pops or Gigi. She learned from the experience and wanted to avoid the potential pain.

My granddaughter's response to pain is natural, but avoiding pain is not a solution in itself. We must also find the source of that pain. One day my daughter was in the process of putting on her shoes when she felt a horrible pain in her toe. She did not sit there thinking, "I wonder why my toe hurts." Or "I wonder if this pain will stop soon." She kicked off her shoe to find what was causing the pain. Lo and behold, inside her shoe there was a hornet! As soon as she identified the source of her pain, she dealt with it appropriately.

If you have experienced the pain of betrayal, it is not enough to attempt to avoid future pain. As we discussed in the last chapter, our natural ways of avoiding pain may be ultimately harmful. The deep wound of betrayal can derail a person's destiny and may have lifelong and even eternal consequences if not addressed in a healthy way. Satan's plan is not necessarily to kill your body; he really wants to defeat your spirit. He wants to distort the way you look at life and how you interact with people.

Instead of avoiding people because they might betray us one day, we must seek to identify the characteristics of those who tend to betray others. Unfortunately this is not easy. Betrayers don't wear signs announcing that they can't be trusted. But there are some common threads that can identify a potential betrayer.

Betrayers Are Self-Seeking

And when Jesus was in Bethany at the house of Simon the leper, a woman came to Him having an alabaster flask of very costly fragrant oil, and she poured it on His head as He sat at the table. But when His disciples saw it, they were indignant, saying, "Why this waste? For this fragrant oil might have been sold for much and given to the poor." But when Jesus was aware of it, He said to them, "Why do you trouble the woman? For she has done a good work for Me. For you have the poor with you always, but Me you do not have always. For in pouring this fragrant oil on My body, she did it for My burial. Assuredly, I say to you, wherever this gospel is preached in the whole world, what this woman has done will also be told as a memorial to her."

—MATTHEW 26:6–13

In this passage of Scripture, we find Jesus and His disciples having a meal at the home of Simon the leper. Mary walked in and began to pour a very expensive flask of perfume over the head of Jesus. More than likely, this perfume was her dowry. The disciples who were with Jesus knew the value of this perfume and that Mary essentially was giving Jesus her future.

Judas was present and had been given charge of the finances. But he was not only funding the ministry, he was also taking a little money for himself. Judas was stealing what had been given to the poor. He was greedy, and his conscience had been seared. He was no longer sensitive to the voice of God; he had become hardened.

When Mary began to pour the alabaster box of oil on Jesus, He received the gift she was giving. Judas, however, became indignant. Watching from the sidelines, he did not see the gift as Jesus saw it; Judas saw *his* money being wasted.

Very often I come into contact with people who do not like the fact that our church gives a large amount of money to missions. They do not like money going to other ministries and feel that it should stay in the local church. They may actually say that we have needy people here and that we should take care of our own church and then worry about everybody else.

Jesus said that we are to take care of the hungry, naked, destitute, and the poor. He said, "Inasmuch as you did it to one of the least of these My brethren, you did it to Me" (Matt. 25:40). He wanted us to take care of others, not just ourselves.

True stewardship is taking care of something for someone else. God gives us gifts and talents to "steward," or take care of for Him. A betrayer does not want to take care of God's gifts for others; he wants them all for himself.

I once brought on a new staff member at a church. Because of the nature of his responsibilities, we asked for a five-year commitment from him. He agreed to our terms and moved into his position, and the turmoil began immediately. At first there was just a feeling of unrest among the staff members, but after a short time there was great discord. Support staff began resigning, and new people were brought on staff.

I began to notice that the new staff member was forming alliances and causing dissension among the current staff. When I began to test whether his heart was to serve the ministry or accomplish his own agenda, he immediately "jumped ship" and moved to another position in another state. He had been on our staff only ten months. This former staff member wanted to use his position to promote himself. He did not want to be part of a staff or to be a steward of what God was doing in the congregation. Betrayers will always have a perverted sense of stewardship.

Snared by Greed

Judas knew the religious leaders did not like Jesus. He knew that they were looking for an opportunity to arrest Jesus and end His influence among the people. In Matthew 26 Judas, who must have been entertaining the idea of betrayal, went to the chief priests to put the process of the betrayal into action. He started it after he was given money.

Then one of the twelve, called Judas Iscariot, went to the chief priests and said, "What are you willing to give me if I deliver Him to you?" And they counted out to him thirty pieces of silver. So from that time he sought opportunity to betray Him.

—MATTHEW 26:14–16

When there is a thief in the house, that thief will always want more. The Bible says greed is never satisfied.

See, the enemy is puffed up; his desires are not upright— but the righteous person will live by his faithfulness— indeed, wine betrays him; he is arrogant and never at rest. Because he is as greedy as the grave and like death is never satisfied, he gathers to himself all the nations and takes captive all the peoples.

—HABAKKUK 2:4–5, NIV

All betrayal starts with greed. A spirit of greed can quickly come into anyone's life and begin to control his or her steward-ship. How do we guard against the spirit of greed? We give. We tithe. When you tithe, you are saying, "God, You own everything I have, and I will not allow a spirit of greed into my life."

There are spirits that we allow to come into our lives willfully and those we never see coming. Would you ever sit down with your children and watch pornography, thereby opening a door to sexual perversion in your family? Knowing that the spirit of pornography destroys and perverts, you would guard against it, would you not? You would make sure it does not have access into your home. You would put a filter on your Internet service and a lock on certain television programming. How do you keep a spirit of greed out of your life? You guard against it by freely giving to God.

The Bible does not tell us much about Judas's background. We do not know if he came from a wealthy family or from humble means. We can surmise that there was something in his life that made him feel as if he needed more than what he had.

When God gives us little blessings and we are faithful with them, He gives us more for which to be accountable. We see this demonstrated in Matthew 25 in the parable of the talents:

> For the kingdom of heaven is like a man traveling to a far country, who called his own servants and delivered his goods to them. And to one he gave five talents, to another two, and to another one, to each according to his own ability; and immediately he went on a journey. Then he who had received the five talents went and traded with them, and made another five talents. And likewise he who had received two gained two more also. But he who had received one went and dug in the ground, and hid his lord's money. After a long time the lord of those servants came and settled accounts with them.
>
> So he who had received five talents came and brought five other talents, saying, "Lord, you delivered to me five talents; look, I have gained five more talents besides them." His lord said to him, "Well done, good and faithful servant; you were faithful over a few things, I will make you ruler over many things. Enter into the joy of your lord." He also who had received two talents came and said, "Lord, you delivered to me two talents; look, I have gained two more talents besides them." His lord said to him, "Well done, good and faithful servant; you have been faithful over a few things, I will make you ruler over many things. Enter into the joy of your lord."
>
> Then he who had received the one talent came and said, "Lord, I knew you to be a hard man, reaping where

you have not sown, and gathering where you have not scattered seed. And I was afraid, and went and hid your talent in the ground. Look, there you have what is yours."

But his lord answered and said to him, "You wicked and lazy servant, you knew that I reap where I have not sown, and gather where I have not scattered seed. So you ought to have deposited my money with the bankers, and at my coming I would have received back my own with interest. Therefore take the talent from him, and give it to him who has ten talents."

—MATTHEW 25:14–28

The servants who were given two talents and five talents doubled them for the master. When they were faithful over them, God gave them more. The servant who was given only one talent hoarded what God gave him and did nothing to increase that gift. His greed caused everything to be taken away from him and given to another. He was called both wicked and lazy.

It is a wicked and lazy thing to hoard a talent God gives us. It does not matter what has motivated us to hoard what God has given us. Greed is sin no matter what the cause.

God is honored when we use the talents He gives us for His glory. In this way He knows we are good stewards, which motivates Him to bless us with more. When Jelly and I were just married and in school, we could not afford anything other than basic necessities. We counted every penny and every dime. We looked under the cushions on our couch and under car seats to find just a little change. We had a written budget, but it really did not matter. There was never enough to meet the budget anyway! We were faithful to God in our tithes and offerings, and He blessed us with more. By the time we finished college, we had a very small nest egg and a job offer, and we were in debt for only a school bill.

When you are faithful with "more," God can bless you with "much." When you are blessed with "much," you walk into a precarious place because "much" means you have many options. "Much" means you don't live paycheck to paycheck; you can plan for the future; you can make purchases without worrying whether ends will meet at the end of the month. This is where people are greatly tested. When we have been blessed with much, we can lose faith, thinking our financial blessings are due to our own hard work and wisdom. Or we can be further elevated by continuing to be faithful with the blessings God gives us.

In Matthew 19:16 a rich young ruler came to Jesus. He had money, position, and youth, but he knew he needed something more from God. When he came to Jesus he asked, "Lord, how do I inherit eternal life?" Jesus essentially said, "Go sell all that you have and give it to the poor and come and follow Me."

Jesus did not tell everyone to do that. The only reason He told the rich young ruler to do that is because Jesus knew the god of the rich young ruler was his money, position, and youth. Jesus continued by telling him that if he were willing to surrender *everything* to God that in this life and in the life to come, he would reap a hundredfold in wealth and riches. Jesus was telling the rich young man, "Put Me first and trust Me, and I will bless you if you allow Me to do so." But the Bible says the rich young ruler went away sorrowful because he had much wealth.

When we are blessed by God, we may forget about the days when we had very little. Do you remember where you were and where God has brought you from?

There is a chain of stores across the United States called Hobby Lobby. David Green is the CEO. When David was growing up, his parents were poor Pentecostal preachers who had very little materially. He started Hobby Lobby in his garage. As the store began to grow and he acquired more and more wealth, David and his family decided that they did not want greed to enter their home. They understood God did not bless them to hoard wealth but to be a blessing to the kingdom of God.

They started finding ways to give. Whenever they found someone or something to support, David and his children and grandchildren would gather together to decide how to give the money. In doing this, he showed his family how to guard against greed. David was faithful with little, and God gave him more. He taught his family how to give and protect themselves from greed and now they have been blessed with much. With "much" they are able to give away millions of dollars every year to support the kingdom.[1]

A friend of mine was once an executive vice president for a moving company in the Southeast. Through his association with the company, my friend became acquainted with the owner and founder. After a time the owner of the company began to give more and more of his company away to his children. After observing some of the changes taking place within the company, my friend asked the owner if he was sure he wanted the changes to continue. This man believed so much in the integrity of his children that he *knew* they would never do anything to hurt him. My friend tried to warn the owner that his family would take away everything he had built, but the man would not listen. Just as my friend feared, there came a day when this affluent man went to work and found that he had been locked out of his own building. His children had turned against him because the spirit of greed began to control them.

Many of us have heard Aesop's Fables. Although they are

thousands of years old, many of the stories are still relevant today. This is one story about greed that bears repeating: There was once a dog who had been given a bone by the local butcher. The dog took the bone in his mouth and began to hurry home. On his way home, he crossed a bridge and happened to look down into the water. There he saw another dog with a much larger bone in his mouth. He wanted the larger bone, so he dropped his own bone and jumped down into the water to take away the larger bone. As he was swimming to the shore, he realized that what he saw was only a reflection and that he had foolishly thrown away what he had. The dog learned the lesson that it is very foolish to be greedy.

Whom Do You Serve?

In Matthew 26:14–16 we see that Judas expected to be paid thirty pieces of silver for betraying Jesus. This was a very small amount of money. Some estimates say that in today's market the silver was worth only four hundred dollars. Judas was willing to go to such extremes for such a small amount because mammon was his god. Serving false gods paves the road to betrayal.

If your god is sex, you will be willing to betray your marriage partner in order to serve your desire. If your god is prestige, you will step on your best friend to get to the next position. If your god is money, you will sell your integrity, your character, or even your family for more. Those who betray bring intentional pain in service of their gods. Their betrayal is rooted in idolatry.

Tiger Woods, revered as the world's greatest golfer, betrayed his wife and family when he broke his marriage vows. He valued personal gratification more than his family. Before his betrayal became public, everything he touched seemed to turn to gold.

Afterward he lost not only his marriage but also millions in cancelled endorsement contracts and untold goodwill.

Lance Armstrong, seven-time winner of the Tour de France, was banned from cycling after admitting to using performance enhancing drugs. Armstrong betrayed his sport through his cheating. Not only has he been banned from professional cycling for the rest of his life, but he was also sued over the millions of dollars spent to sponsor his cycling team. Armstrong valued his standing more than the integrity of his sport and hurt his supporters in the process.

Judas's betrayal was premeditated and was intended to cause Jesus's death. Peter's failure, on the other hand, was based on the weakness of his flesh. Remember, Peter failed; he didn't betray. If we are not careful, we will put people who have failed in the same category with people who betray. One critical difference is that betrayal is premeditated and brings intentional hurt.

Jesus told Judas that it would have been better for him if he had not been born. Jesus knew what Judas was planning to do (John 6:70–71). To Peter He said, "Satan has asked for you, that he may sift you as wheat. But I have prayed for you, that your faith should not fail" (Luke 22:31–32). Do you see the difference? After Jesus died on the cross and rose from the dead, He went looking for Peter in order to restore him.

I want to stress this point because you may have treated someone who failed you as if he betrayed you when in fact he failed you. People who fail us shouldn't be cast aside; we should seek to restore the relationship. Those who have failed their friends and loved ones need to be loved and brought back into fellowship. Those who have betrayed, on the other hand, need to be forgiven but not given the opportunity to betray again.

Betrayal is premeditated; it is intentional. Failure is a weakness of the flesh. Failure happens because we are human.

It may be tempting to seek to restore a betrayer, but betrayers need a cataclysmic event to prompt them to change. A cataclysmic event is something momentous and violent; it is marked by overwhelming upheaval and demolition. In order for a betrayer to change, something significant has to happen in his or her life. Usually it must be public in order for him to admit his wrongdoing.

Betrayers Don't Show Respect

In John 13:23–30 Jesus was having the Passover meal, one of the most holy meals for a Jewish person. After His three-and-a-half years of ministry, three-and-a-half years of miracles, and thirty-three years of sinless living, Jesus was to partake of this final covenantal meal. His time had come. More than likely Jesus was already beginning to feel the weight of what was coming. There must have been an incredible weight on Him spiritually as both heaven and hell anticipated what Jesus was about to do.

> One of them, the disciple whom Jesus loved, was reclining next to him. Simon Peter motioned to this disciple and said, "Ask him which one he means."
>
> Leaning back against Jesus, he asked him, "Lord, who is it?"
>
> Jesus answered, "It is the one to whom I will give this piece of bread when I have dipped it in the dish." Then, dipping the piece of bread, he gave it to Judas Iscariot, son of Simon Iscariot. As soon as Judas took the bread, Satan entered into him.
>
> So Jesus told him, "What you are about to do, do

quickly." But no one at the meal understood why Jesus said this to him. Since Judas had charge of the money, some thought Jesus was telling him to buy what was needed for the festival, or to give something to the poor. As soon as Judas had taken the bread, he went out. And it was night.

—JOHN 13:23–30, NIV

Even in such a tense spiritual atmosphere, Judas chose to betray Jesus. Even if a person is in a spiritual environment, that does not mean he could never betray. It is hard for many people to believe that someone who attends church regularly, sings in the choir, or is in leadership could possibly betray. But the fact is, even if you are in the most intense spiritual environment, if your heart is not right with God, the presence of God has no effect on you.

In verse 23 of the passage above, we see that the disciples were reclining at the table. This was common practice in biblical times.

By the time of JESUS, the Roman custom of reclining on couches at supper had been adopted in some Jewish circles. The Roman table and couches combined was called a triclinium. There were three couches which were located on the three sides of a square, the fourth side being left open, so that a servant could get on the inside to assist in serving the meal. The guest's position was to recline with the body's upper part resting on the left arm, and the head raised, and a cushion at the back, and the lower part of the body stretched out. The head of the second guest was opposite the breast of the first guest, so that if he wanted to speak to him in secret he would lean upon his breast.[2]

As John leaned against the breast of Jesus and asked who it was that was betraying Him, all of the disciples, according to customs, were reclining at the table. Jesus gave the bread to Judas, Satan entered into Judas, and Jesus told Judas to go quickly to complete his task. Although it is not stated as such, it is implied that Judas stood up at this point, indicating that he was ready to leave. This was an act of disrespect to the Master. It was a small, but obvious show of Judas's disdain.

I think it is important to note that Judas stood up when Jesus confirmed his betrayal, which was an act of disrespect. You may begin to notice a lack of respect from your betrayer. It may be interrupting you in conversation, taking or making telephone calls during meetings, referring to you on a first-name basis when you have asked otherwise, having insulting humor, or showing contempt for your ideas and decisions. Maybe you have asked that something be completed, and it has not been done. Excuses may be made, but the bottom line is that it was just not important enough to the betrayer to honor your requests. These are all indications that something is happening in the person's heart that could lead him or her to betray you.

In the Rodgers and Hammerstein play *The King and I* Anna was instructed to always keep her head below the king of Siam's. This was how Anna was to show him respect. Anna said she would try to honor this directive, but she would not grovel on the floor. The king then stood up and called her a difficult woman. He got her to promise to keep her head as low as his and then proceeded to test her. He knelt down, she sat on the floor. He rested on an elbow and then waited for her to get lower than him. Anna began to understand that she was to give honor and respect to the king of Siam. Though humorous, this scene illustrates Anna's desire to honor the king.

Honor is something that is sadly missing in our society. The word *honor* means to hold someone in esteem or to regard with respect. This is something we do not always see. Men walk ahead of women and don't open doors for them; children talk back to parents and educators; women publicly belittle their husbands; and elected officials abuse the very laws they have sworn to uphold. Betrayers often have a hard time honoring the authority God has placed in their lives, and as a result they often do not yield to correction. A person who does not respect others will seek to satisfy their own needs even if it means hurting someone else.

Chapter 5

CHARACTERISTICS OF A JUDAS

SOME OF YOU who are reading this book have been divorced. Others of you have been gravely wounded by your children. Still others have almost been devastated by your parents, a sibling, or another family member. Some of you have been betrayed by an employer or employee. You may have been physically abused by a spouse or another loved one. This can be the hardest betrayal to face—when the very ones who should keep you safe are the ones who put you in danger.

Betrayal has become so prevalent in our society that there is now a psychological theory called "betrayal trauma." *Trauma* is defined as a deeply distressing or disturbing experience or an emotional shock following a stressful event. Betrayal trauma occurs when a person is significantly dependent on another person for his well-being and his trust is violated. An example of this would be when a child, dependent on his parents for sustenance, is abused by those parents in some manner. When the betrayer is a caregiver or needed other, the betrayal can influence the way the trauma is remembered. It is thought that if the person is blind to the betrayal, he will be more likely to survive the experience. If the person becomes aware of the betrayal, he will struggle with the subsequent emotional responses and may even be debilitated by them.

Allow me to pause here and express an important point: if you are being abused, you need to get to a safe place. God does not expect you to live with someone who is harming you or your children. I once had a minister friend who told me about his counseling ministry. He said that one of his parishioners came to him in distress because her husband was beating her. He told her to have her husband come to visit him and he would see if he could help.

A few days later the man entered into the pastor's office and sat down. The pastor moved his chair very close to the husband and told him why he needed to see him. He then asked the husband why he would hit a woman. The husband said, "Because I felt like it."

My friend the pastor drew his hand back and slapped the husband across the face, telling him, "I just felt like doing that." He then drew back his other hand, slapped him again and said, "I just felt like doing that too."

The husband was flabbergasted that the pastor would slap him, but the pastor got his message across. He then told the husband, "If you ever feel like hitting your wife again, I think the spirit of slap will come all over me again."

Years later he saw the couple at an event and began to converse with them. According to the wife, her husband had never again used physical violence toward her and they were now happily married. Sometimes the betrayer needs to be reminded of the difference between right and wrong. Abuse is always wrong.

Real People With Real Problems

One of the things I love about the Bible is that it is full of stories about real people who had real problems. They all had choices to make about how to deal with those problems. Some people were successful overcomers and some were not. Some forgave and some became bitter. Those who became bitter were unable to do anything significant for God. Those who faced betrayal and forgave did mighty works for God.

Joseph had a father who loved him deeply. He also had eleven brothers who did not. His brothers hated him so much that they sold him into slavery.

> So Joseph went after his brothers and found them near Dothan. But they saw him in the distance, and before he reached them, they plotted to kill him. "Here comes that dreamer!" they said to each other. "Come now, let's kill him and throw him into one of these cisterns and say that a ferocious animal devoured him. Then we'll see what comes of his dreams." When Reuben heard this, he tried to rescue him from their hands. "Let's not take his life," he said. "Don't shed any blood. Throw him into this cistern here in the wilderness, but don't lay a hand on him." Reuben said this to rescue him from them and take him back to his father. So when Joseph came to his brothers, they stripped him of his robe—the ornate robe he was wearing—and they took him and threw him into the cistern. The cistern was empty; there was no water in it.
> —GENESIS 37:17–24, NIV

Many years after Joseph was sold into slavery, he met his brothers again. Joseph could have had every one of them executed, but he chose to forgive and bless them instead. Joseph recognized the hand of God in all that had happened to him and made sure that his brothers knew it too. In Genesis Joseph states:

> And God sent me before you to preserve a posterity for you in the earth, and to save your lives by a great deliverance. So now it was not you who sent me here, but God; and He has made me a father to Pharaoh, and lord of all his house, and a ruler throughout all the land of Egypt.
> —GENESIS 45:7–8

Joseph had truly forgiven his brothers and as a result was able to save their lives and the lives of their families. The destiny of the people in your life may be dependent on your ability to overcome betrayal. We will discuss that idea in later chapters.

In Genesis 9 we find the story of Noah who was betrayed by his son. Ham mocked his father and exposed his nakedness, the height of dishonor and disrespect. As a result, Noah cursed Ham and he became a "servant of servants."

> When he drank some of its wine, he became drunk and lay uncovered inside his tent. Ham, the father of Canaan, saw his father naked and told his two brothers outside. But Shem and Japheth took a garment and laid it across their shoulders; then they walked in backward and covered their father's naked body. Their faces were turned the other way so that they would not see their father naked. When Noah awoke from his wine and found out what his youngest son had done to him, he said, "Cursed be Canaan! The lowest of slaves will he be to his brothers."
> —GENESIS 9:21–25, NIV

Samson, one of the greatest judges of Israel, found his betrayer in a woman he loved, Delilah (Judg. 16:15–21). She questioned him about the source of his strength again and again, and each time Samson would tease her with an invalid answer. When she was finally able to get him to share his heart with her, she betrayed him. I have never understood why Samson told her the real source of his strength after she'd tested every answer he'd given her. It may be that Samson thought he was indestructible.

Elisha had a servant named Gehazi who betrayed him for financial gain (2 Kings 5:20–27). Elisha confronted him and told Gehazi that "his spirit" had gone with him when Gehazi took money from Naaman. Elisha loved Gehazi, but Gehazi loved possessions more.

Even the apostle Paul faced the heartbreak of betrayal when he stated in his letter to Timothy that Demas had forsaken him.

> Be diligent to come to me quickly; for Demas has forsaken me, having loved this present world, and has departed for Thessalonica—Crescens for Galatia, Titus for Dalmatia. Only Luke is with me. Get Mark and bring him with you, for he is useful to me for ministry.
> —2 TIMOTHY 4:9–11

Since betrayal comes in so many different forms, knowing the general characteristics of a Judas will help you protect yourself from future betrayals.

A Judas Is Self-Serving

A Judas may seem spiritual on the outside, but his commitment to Christ is often in name only. A Judas will be in the choir, on the praise team, on the board of elders, part of the usher ministry, a Sunday school teacher, or even a pastoral staff member. A betrayer may even have spiritual gifts that are used publicly. He or she will appear to have a deep, personal walk with Christ, but they really desire something else.

There once was a woman in our church whose unsaved husband had been unfaithful to her in the early years of their marriage. He eventually came to know Jesus Christ as his Savior and became involved in various ministries of the church. He became a good man, a good father, grandfather, and provider. She appeared to be a godly woman and seemed to have a dynamic prayer ministry. She made it her goal in life to let everyone know that God can restore anyone. But she did this by sharing details of her husband's unfaithfulness and her hurt as a result of it. This was usually done in a group setting.

Although she masked it as ministry, this woman was a gossip. She really did not care if people knew God could restore them. She just wanted everyone to know that her husband had been unfaithful and had caused her great heartache. She wanted everyone to see what he had been before he came to Christ. She was not interested in them seeing the godly man he had become. She betrayed her husband every time she threw the past in his face to elicit sympathy for herself.

A Judas Is Manipulative

Judases can be extremely practical and may seem to be good problem solvers. The word *practical* means something of, relating to, or manifested in practice or action rather than theory, speculation, or ideals. Betrayers may earn your trust by appearing to be good at dealing with difficulties. But they will help you solve problems to serve their own purposes. A true Judas can manipulate you into doing what they want you to do while thinking it was your own idea.

I once had a staff member who was a Judas. If I had an issue with a particular person in the church, I went to this individual. My betrayer had been in the church for many years and convinced me that he knew how to handle the person. I found myself asking this person to take care of things someone else could have easily done because I trusted him. I felt safe asking for help. This is how the individual got close enough to manipulate situations for personal benefit and ultimately to betray me.

A Judas Is a Thief

In John 12 Mary anoints Jesus with a fragrant perfume that was very expensive. The woman's actions were prophetically significant, because they were preparing Jesus for His death. But Judas's reaction to the woman is revealing.

> But one of his disciples, Judas Iscariot, who was later to betray him, objected, "Why wasn't this perfume sold and the money given to the poor? It was worth a year's wages." He did not say this because he cared about the poor but because he was a thief; as keeper of the money bag, he used to help himself to what was put into it.
> —JOHN 12:4–6, NIV

A betrayer will steal from you. A Judas will take your time, money, and influence. The Scripture says Satan comes to steal, kill, and destroy (John 10:10)! Betrayers carry out the work of the original betrayer, Satan. Though a created being, Satan thought he could steal heaven from the one who created it. Satan is still in the business of theft.

We once had an usher in our church who was a thief. I considered this man a friend. He had been in the church for a few months when he volunteered to be an usher. He was friendly, and everyone enjoyed being around him. One of his favorite things to say was, "You trust me, don't you? You know I'm going to take care of you."

At this point allow me to give you a nugget of truth: if anyone ever asks you to trust him, don't. A person of integrity does not need to ask you to trust him.

After our offerings were received, we took them to a room to be counted. There were always three or four people in the room for the sake of accountability. When the offerings were counted, they were recorded and then placed in a safe until the next business day.

After my friend started working with the ushering staff, we began to notice that there were no longer any bills in our offerings that were larger than twenty dollars. We also began receiving calls from various people saying their giving records were not accurate. Puzzled, we installed a secret camera and then placed some marked bills in the Pastor's Appreciation Day offering. The offering was brought into the room and counted.

As we watched the recording we saw the usher shuffle the money around and hide the marked bills in his coat pockets. A Las Vegas card dealer would have been proud to see how easily this friend of mine moved those bills out of sight. Even when he was confronted with the evidence of his theft, he denied that he had taken any money. He even had the temerity to ask me at that point if I did not trust him to do the right thing. It was only after the threat of prosecution that he returned the money stolen from that offering.

This Judas also had a business at which my wife and I had a personal account. In this business he also did some maintenance work on our vehicles. At that time Jelly's car was very old and had quite a few things wrong with it. We took it repeatedly to the business to be repaired, but the problems were never resolved or something else went wrong with it. After he was caught with his hand in the proverbial cookie jar, we began to cross-reference our bills with the actual work that had been done. We found that not only had the work not been done, but we also had been double charged in some instances. The repairs that were not completed could have caused a horrible accident in which Jelly and the children could have been gravely injured. Not only had he stolen from God's house, but he had also put the lives of my family at risk.

A Judas Is a Deceiver

To deceive means to mislead by a false appearance or statement, to delude, or to be unfaithful. Someone who is a betrayer will always try to mislead for personal gain.

I have a friend who is the president of a nonprofit organization that feeds, educates, and medically assists children in another country. After he took charge of the organization, he found that there were some things he just could not do alone. He brought in a friend as a consultant to help him organize and streamline the domestic side of the organization.

During the reorganization, he contracted another man to raise funds and a young lady to work with the financial arm of the ministry. Soon he began to sense that something was not right in the organization but could not determine exactly what was wrong. He took two of the three people he had hired on an overseas trip to observe the inner workings of the ministry. Due to the distance and length of the trip, it cost the organization almost $12,000.

Over the next two months he found that projects were not being completed, jobs were being shifted, and policy changes that he had not approved were being implemented. He also found that office personnel were being asked to complete personal assignments for one of the men. The ministry was preparing for a large event when he received the resignations of both men and the young woman. It appeared that both the event and the office were deliberately put into peril. Fortunately there were others who could step in and complete the tasks of those who had resigned.

After their resignations, he found that the young lady had given proprietary information to the man who had been contracted to streamline the office. She gave him passwords and confidential documents, and she did it from her home computer! This was not just an act of betrayal, but it was also illegal.

The deception was deliberate and motivated by greed. The consultant was using the other two staff members in his personal business. My friend felt that this violated the code of ethics by which he lived and that he had been betrayed by people he trusted.

A Judas will try to mislead you. Deception is the practice of deliberately trying to get somebody to believe things that are not true. Allowing somebody to believe even a half-truth is deception. If you allow somebody to believe something that is not true, you are a part of the deception. This makes you a deceiver.

If you buy an item and wear it, and then attempt to return it because you never removed the store tags, that is deception. If you purchase an item and get it dirty before you can use it, then take it back as if the stain occurred in the store, that is deception. If you are speeding down the road and then act as though you didn't realize you were over the limit when a police officer pulls you over, that is deception. All of these are deceptions and lay the groundwork for a future as a betrayer.

A deceiver will lie when the truth would be a better story. He deceives when there is no reason to do so. He will embellish an incident to his credit. A Judas may not be blatant in his deception. He may not tell an outright lie. He may tell a white lie, a lie that in his mind hurts no one. He may tell of something you said or did and leave out some information that will distort the truth of the matter.

The deception and the thievery will not occur until Judas is deeply planted in your life. You will not see the deceiver because you look for truth, not lies. Frank Abagnale is considered one of the top ten impostors in America. He spent many years masquerading as a pilot, a doctor, and an attorney. He was a master forger. He was so good, in fact, that after he was caught and incarcerated for five years, he was paroled on the condition that he would work with the government to help catch check forgers.

Abagnale started his life of deception with petty crimes as a teenager. He cost his parents thousands of dollars with one of his credit card schemes and nearly cost the life of a child in Georgia while masquerading as a doctor. His deception ended more than forty years ago, but that is still what he is best known for, especially after it was chronicled in the movie *Catch Me If You Can*.

No one wants to face betrayal, but most people will. Rather than shielding yourself from the world, keep yourself open and watch for the characteristics we have discussed in this and the previous chapter. Betrayal is not inevitable. You can take steps to safeguard yourself.

Chapter 6

A PERSONAL LESSON IN BETRAYAL

M Y FIRST PASTORATE was in a small town in Georgia. Jelly and
I were very young and naïve. Jelly had grown up in a pastor's
home, so she knew some of the pitfalls of ministry. She had
seen the good side of ministry as well as the bad. Her mother
and father had taken troubled churches and brought them into
health again. She knew that church people were among the most
generous, loving, gentle, and kind people in the world. She also
knew that people in churches could be very unkind and could
bite the very hands that fed them. She had experienced firsthand
both ends of the spectrum. The ugly side made her sure she did
not want any part of the ministry, but God had a different idea.

I had grown up in a military home and knew very little about
ministry aside from leading a small youth group. At that time
ministering to teens was the most fun I had ever had in life. I
could play with them, eat with them, pour godly principles into
them, love them, and watch them love me back. I mistakenly
thought that churches were similar to the military. If a pastor
said something was supposed to be done in a certain way, then

it should be that way. In the military you were never supposed to question those in authority. My wife and I came from two entirely different places, and we tried to put the two perspectives together. Our approach worked for the most part...until it didn't.

Our church was small and had a history of problems. The entire town had revolving doors on pastors' homes. There was always someone leaving and someone arriving. I was the church's only pastoral candidate, and Jelly and I were unanimously voted in. Of course, there were only about twenty-five people voting! We made plans to move to Georgia to be senior pastors. Little did I know that we were not just the only candidates but quite possibly the church's last option. Had we not accepted the position, the church would have closed its doors. Although I was not 100 percent sure this was where God was leading, we packed everything we owned in a truck and headed east with all our stuff, a new baby, and an irritated cat.

Our first Sunday was April 1, commonly known as April Fools' Day. There were times when I wondered if God was somehow joking with me to allow my new ministry post to begin on that day. When our first service began, I kept waiting for the people to come in and then realized they were all there. The song service began—notice that I did not say the "praise and worship" service began—and it felt as if I had gone back in time at least ten years. The songs were that old. I could tell this was going to be a long Sunday morning. The congregation was unsure of this kid pastor, and on top of everything our baby kept crying and there was no nursery. With so many things going wrong, I wondered if I had somehow missed God's leading.

As Jelly and I became more confident and established our leadership, we saw life creep into the sanctuary. The church people began to smile at one another and after a time, we changed the song service to praise and worship.

This was back when churches were first starting to use overhead projectors to display the lyrics to the praise and worship songs. We decided to do this too. On the third Sunday in our new church, we projected the lyrics on the wall and started singing more contemporary music. A lady who attended the church became so angry that she left the service. Her husband later came to me and said that she would not be back because we were showing movies in the church. I was confused until he explained that since we put up a projector, we were showing movies.

It sounded very trite then and sounds very ridiculous now. I remember thinking that I had inadvertently stirred up a hornet's nest. Jelly and I decided to visit the woman to try to correct the situation. When you have only twenty-five people in the church, you cannot afford to lose anybody. Dogs and cats count when you have twenty-five people. Pigs count when you have twenty-five people. Everyone and everything is welcome when you have twenty-five people in the church.

Later that week Jelly and I went for an afternoon pastoral visit. It was around 2:30, just before her children got home from school. We walked up to the door, and I was just about to knock on the door when I realized that the television was tuned to a trashy soap opera. There was a nasty scene being played out, and I held out my hand to stop Jelly from coming any closer. I whispered to her, "Ooh, this is not nice. You can go wait in the car if you want to, but I am going to stand here and see how long this will continue."

The scene on the television started getting worse, and I could see through the screen door that she was absolutely mesmerized by what she was watching. Jelly told me that I shouldn't watch her, but I said, "I'm just here for a pastoral visit. It is not my fault that she left the door open and I can see through the screen." Jelly gave me one of those "this is not what a pastor is supposed to do" looks. Remember, I don't know anything about being a pastor. She's the pastor's daughter.

I continued to watch and at the next commercial, knocked loudly on the screened door. She jumped up off the couch like Catwoman and was extremely surprised to see me standing there. She asked how long I had been there, and I told her, "Long enough. I'll see you in church on Wednesday, won't I?"

Her eyes were as big as saucers as she said, "Yeah."

I said, "You won't complain anymore about us singing Scripture songs and projecting them up on the wall either, will you?"

She dropped her head and said, "No."

"OK," I said, "I just wanted to be sure we had a good understanding."

As far as I was concerned, that was the end of the problem. It would never be necessary to bring it up again.

Over the next few years I know there were times when she wanted to say or do something negative, but somehow she resisted. I will not say that she felt threatened or blackmailed in any way, but she had learned a very difficult lesson. After our soap opera encounter, I could have gotten up the next Sunday and said unkind and hurtful things. I chose to not do that because I knew she was simply misguided. A Judas is not misguided. A Judas is intentional in bringing about your destruction. You always need to determine if your betrayal stems from someone who is misguided or is intentionally hurtful.

The church began to grow and we began to develop leaders.

One Sunday morning a very confident couple came to our church and told me they had been searching for a new church and had decided that this was to be their new church home. They wanted to be put to work immediately. They were an answer to my prayers for God to send us leaders. Beth* was a pastor's daughter and knew all the pressures of ministry. Her husband, Tim,* was former military so it seemed like they were created to walk alongside Jelly and me.

Although they were quite a bit older, their backgrounds were so similar to ours that I immediately let down my guard. I felt they had been sent by God to help us do what He wanted in this little north Georgia town. They both had much experience working in churches and already knew our doctrines. There was no need for them to go through a membership class or any kind of assimilation, or so I thought. They began teaching some of our Christian education classes. They sang in the choir. If they saw anything that needed to be done, they would be the first to do it.

We struggled in those first years and just when things looked the bleakest, Beth and Tim would call and invite us to lunch at their little home in the mountains. If we could break away, we would pack our children in the car (by this time, we had two) and drive twenty minutes away for an afternoon of total relaxation. We would walk through their woods. Our children would pet their animals, and we would unload our troubles to them. They told us, "This conversation would never go anywhere else, Pastor. You can trust us." They slipped under our guard.

---

* Not their real names.

Disaster Strikes

Our church kept growing, and we eventually outgrew our sanctuary and started building a new building. We had just put up the office section when a tornado came through our little town and destroyed our new building. It hit our day care facility, the current sanctuary, and two other buildings. No one was injured, but the damage was extensive, and many in the community were emotionally traumatized.

Network television stations arrived and began to film the damage as we started the cleanup. For two days we had no electricity and no phone service, but both were restored in time for our church services. Because we'd had no telephone service, we had no way to call anyone had we even thought about it. Cell phones were not widely used in those days and a two-minute long distance call was a luxury we could not afford.

Tim and Beth arrived on Sunday morning in anger because we had not personally let them know what was happening at the church. They felt I should have called them or driven to see them so that they would know what was transpiring at the church. They thought I should have dropped everything because they were so important to the work of the Lord. They said they were experienced in disaster preparedness and would have been invaluable to our efforts. I tried, to no avail, to explain my reasons. The more I talked the angrier they became. We were at an impasse. This is when the trouble began.

What I did not know when they first arrived at our church was that they were leaving the other church due to the pastor's "ineptitude." They had worked their way through all of the charismatic churches in their county and had decided to travel one county north to our church. Oh, what a blessing! As a leader

I learned a very important principle: if they leave wrong, they arrive wrong. If there is a problem that is not resolved when the person resigns their position or if they get angry and leave the church, the anger and the frustration will follow them to the new place and will remain with them until they choose to resolve it.

Tim and Beth began a campaign to let everyone know what a horrible pastor I was. Through all of this I tried to love them back into fellowship. Because of the influence they had among the new members, I was reluctant to correct or rebuke them. They continued to sing in the choir, but their attitudes were polluting the ministry. They sat in the choir with scowls on their faces and scoffed at almost everything I said. They made a great show of leaving before I began to preach, exiting through the side door at the front of the sanctuary.

For eight months I tried to salvage the relationship, but they were unwilling to admit that they might somehow be wrong. The pain we felt was greater than anything Jelly or I had ever encountered. We felt that we had lost a great friendship. Our children would ask to visit Grandpa Tim and Grandma Beth. They did not understand why we couldn't go, and we could not tell them.

> Even my close friend in whom I trusted, who ate my bread, has lifted his heel against me.
> —PSALM 41:9, ESV

I removed the couple from all leadership positions but not from church membership. When you have betrayers in your midst, you have to allow them to continue in their set paths so they will expose themselves. A true Judas will always expose himself.

A betrayer will not receive private correction so he is ultimately exposed when he is rebuked. Jesus rebuked Judas on several different occasions before Judas betrayed Him:

1. Jesus rebuked Judas for getting angry at Mary when she poured the alabaster of oil on Him.

> But Judas Iscariot, one of his disciples (he who was about to betray him), said, "Why was this ointment not sold for three hundred denarii and given to the poor?" He said this, not because he cared about the poor, but because he was a thief, and having charge of the moneybag he used to help himself to what was put into it.
>
> —JOHN 12:4–6, ESV

2. Judas was rebuked during the Feast of Passover, which was a very intimate time of fellowship among the disciples. They were relaxing and sharing a very pleasant meal. Jesus had just washed their feet and had spoken to them about humility and serving others. After this He identified His betrayer as Judas, one of His very own disciples.

> And as they were reclining at table and eating, Jesus said, "Truly, I say to you, one of you will betray me, one who is eating with me." They began to be sorrowful and to say to him one after another, "Is it I?" He said to them, "It is one of the twelve, one who is dipping bread into the dish with me. For the Son of Man goes as it is written of him, but woe to that man by whom the Son of Man is betrayed! It would have been better for that man if he had not been born."
>
> —MARK 14:18–21, ESV

3. Jesus rebuked Judas after teaching His disciples. Many had deserted Him by this time, and He asked the remaining disciples if they too wanted to leave Him. According to John 6:64, Jesus knew from the beginning who would not believe in Him and who would betray Him. Still, Jesus endeavored to correct Judas through the rebuke and see if his heart would be changed.

After this many of his disciples turned back and no longer walked with him. So Jesus said to the Twelve, "Do you want to go away as well?" Simon Peter answered him, "Lord, to whom shall we go? You have the words of eternal life, and we have believed, and have come to know, that you are the Holy One of God." Jesus answered them, "Did I not choose you, the Twelve? And yet one of you is a devil." He spoke of Judas the son of Simon Iscariot, for he, one of the Twelve, was going to betray him.

—JOHN 6:66–71, ESV

4. Jesus rebuked Judas in the garden when He said, "Does thou betray Me with a kiss?" (See Luke 22:48.)

While he was still speaking, Judas came, one of the twelve, and with him a great crowd with swords and clubs, from the chief priests and the elders of the people. Now the betrayer had given them a sign, saying, "The one I will kiss is the man; seize him." And he came up to Jesus at once and said, "Greetings, Rabbi!" And he kissed him. Jesus said to him, "Friend, do what you came to do." Then they came up and laid hands on Jesus and seized him.

—MATTHEW 26:47–50, ESV

Jesus let it be known that there was a betrayer in their midst because He knew Judas would not respond to His correction. And He knew that Judas would eventually reveal himself as a betrayer. That is what happened with Tim and Beth.

After we removed them from their leadership positions, they wrote a twenty-six page document and sent it to all of our board members, the district officials of our denomination, and the members of our church. They accused me of everything they could imagine. They could not accuse me of anything immoral, but they did say I was a dictator. During this time, they continued to attend church, but their influence was waning.

I never had to tell them to leave the church because, through their actions, they removed themselves. I had removed them from positions of leadership and influence, but I had never asked them to leave the church. It was only after I and a board member confronted them about a particular issue that they chose to leave the church. By this time their actions and attitudes had become so tainted that they had lost all of their influence and many of their friendships within the church.

For twelve months afterward anytime we had a birthday, anniversary, appreciation day, Christmas, vacation, or any special occasion, they would send us a nasty letter with the intent of ruining our celebrations. Each letter would threaten a lawsuit. After one particularly trying day I took all the documents they had mailed to me and gave them to an attorney. The burden I was bearing was becoming too much for me. I was getting discouraged by the constant assault on my time and integrity as a minister. The ordeal was becoming so exhausting I was at the point of giving up ministry and going into secular work.

The attorney read through the documents and quickly told me that Tim and Beth had no grounds for any type of lawsuit against me or the church but that I had a very strong lawsuit against them for defamation of character! I had no plans to pursue the suit, but it was very freeing for me to know that I had my own ammunition. The attorney constructed a letter to send to my former friends, and I never heard from them again.

Speak Up

Walking through this first Judas experience in ministry was one of the hardest things I had ever done in my life. I did not know that Christians could behave in a manner such as they did. I did not know how to deal with the betrayal when it began. It was only after I had walked through it that I was able to see the hand of God showing me one step at a time exactly what to do and how to do it.

If you are in ministry, one of the lessons I want you to take from this chapter is the fact that you probably will not have to remove a true Judas. Their actions will do it for them. If you will stay kind in your spirit, God will fight your battle for you. The time will come for you to take action but you must be careful not to be hasty.

The Book of Galatians explains how to give godly discipline:

> Brethren, if a man is overtaken in any trespass, you who are spiritual restore such a one in a spirit of gentleness, considering yourself lest you also be tempted. Bear one another's burdens, and so fulfill the law of Christ. For if anyone thinks himself to be something, when he is nothing, he deceives himself.
> —GALATIANS 6:1–3

I like the way The Message Bible puts it:

Live creatively, friends. If someone falls into sin, for-
givingly restore him, saving your critical comments for
yourself. You might be needing forgiveness before the
day's out. Stoop down and reach out to those who are
oppressed. Share their burdens, and so complete Christ's
law. If you think you are too good for that, you are badly
deceived.

—GALATIANS 6:1–3

The Bible says that when someone enters into trespass, you
who are spiritual must restore the one who is weak. That means
not every believer is supposed to restore people who have fallen.
That is for the leadership to do. We are all to speak up when we
witness wrongdoing, but according to the apostle Paul the actual
correction, discipline, and restoration should be left to those who
are more spiritual.

This is not to say that only pastors are spiritual. In this case
spiritual is referring to those who are more seasoned in ministry. Someone who has been a parent for fifteen or twenty years
will know a little bit more about parenting than someone who is
just about ready to give birth, right? You can read Dr. Seuss, Dr.
Spock, or any other doctor you want, but until that baby comes
you will not actually know what to do when she starts crying. At
midnight when you are tired and the baby will not go to sleep,
Dr. Spock will not be there. You need to talk to someone who is
experienced.

My wife, Jelly, was a preschool administrator for ten years. She
also taught school and is a mother and grandmother. Sometimes
one of our daughters will call to ask her opinion on a strange
symptom they may have. Her sisters do the same thing. Jelly is
not a doctor; she just has experience. She has been a mother for

a long time, and she has dealt with many issues, so she knows what to do or where to go to get help.

It is in this spirit that we should leave restoration to those who know what they are doing. They are in the business of restoring those who have been hurt, and they know what to do.

When I was about seventeen years old, my pastor was dealing with a situation in the church. I heard an adult talking against my pastor and I confronted him, saying, "Sir, that's rebellion."

He was very offended and asked, "How dare you talk to me like that?"

I replied, "Sir, I'm being polite. I'm just telling you that you are in rebellion. Pastor said that when there is sin we are to tell people they have twenty-four hours to go and make it right with the person. I'm telling you right now, you have twenty-four hours to go make it right with Pastor because I will call him."

This man looked at me like he was a deer in headlights. I had challenged him. He knew he had spoken against the man of God and he needed to make it right. Fortunately, he did.

When someone comes to me and says he saw someone doing something wrong, I always ask if he is ready to confront that person. More often than not, the person is unwilling to do so. The problem with confrontation is that you have to be willing to risk ruining the relationship and any ensuing emotional pain.

When you confront someone, you face the risk of being rejected. In fact, there is a fifty-fifty chance that you will be rejected. You must love someone enough to tell them the truth even if they do not like it. A betrayer's actions will probably cause them to be removed from their position, but you must love them enough to confront them if necessary.

We live in a day and time where people do not want discipline. They want plenty of grace. They say they want us to just forgive and love as Jesus did. Jesus did forgive and love, but He also disciplined. He didn't turn a blind eye to wrongdoing. He drove out those who were disrespecting the house of God. Scripture says Jesus whipped the money changers:

> And He found in the temple those who sold oxen and sheep and doves, and the money changers doing business. When He had made a whip of cords, He drove them all out of the temple, with the sheep and the oxen, and poured out the changers' money and overturned the tables. And He said to those who sold doves, "Take these things away! Do not make My Father's house a house of merchandise!" Then His disciples remembered that it was written, "Zeal for Your house has eaten Me up."
> —JOHN 2:14–17

That is definitely discipline, but it is also grace.

When Jesus was approached with the woman caught in adultery, He told her to go and sin no more. His statement was full of love but it was also firm. We like the love but not the firmness.

> Jesus went across to Mount Olives, but he was soon back in the Temple again. Swarms of people came to him. He sat down and taught them. The religion scholars and Pharisees led in a woman who had been caught in an act of adultery. They stood her in plain sight of everyone and said, "Teacher, this woman was caught red-handed in the act of adultery. Moses, in the Law, gives orders to stone such persons. What do you say?" They were trying to trap him into saying something incriminating so they could bring charges against him. Jesus bent down and wrote with his finger in the dirt. They kept at him, badgering him. He straightened up and said, "The sinless one among you, go first: Throw the stone." Bending

down again, he wrote some more in the dirt. Hearing that, they walked away, one after another, beginning with the oldest. The woman was left alone. Jesus stood up and spoke to her. "Woman, where are they? Does no one condemn you?" "No one, Master." "Neither do I," said Jesus. "Go on your way. From now on, don't sin."
—JOHN 8:1–11, THE MESSAGE

Someone once said that the only people who are mad at you for speaking the truth are those who are living a lie. We are to speak truth and live truth, and speak up when we know something is not truth.

A good parent will discipline when necessary. An unruly or undisciplined child will become a terror to those around him. A good parent will teach a child to take responsibility for his actions, to "own" his failures. That same parent will also teach the child the importance of problem resolution and allow the child to resolve issues that arise within his or her relationships.

When the church operates properly, we discipline. If we don't discipline, we are not operating in the manner God designed us to operate. You can be a part of the Moose Club, the Kiwanis Club, or the Rotary Club and still experience discipline. If you miss a certain number of meetings in a row you are out of the club. It does not matter how much money you have. You have to be there and support the club. If you do not pay the dues, you are out. What I am trying to convey is that most organizations, clubs, and businesses have a code of ethics and a disciplinary process. If they have a disciplinary process, then surely the kingdom should also.

You may not be called to manage the disciplinary process, but we all must speak up when we see wrongdoing. As the apostle Paul wrote: "You must not simply look the other way and hope it goes away on its own. Bring it out in the open and deal with it in the authority of Jesus our Master. Assemble the community—I'll be present in spirit with you and our Master Jesus will be present in power. Hold this man's conduct up to public scrutiny. Let him defend it if he can! But if he can't, then out with him! It will be totally devastating to him, of course, and embarrassing to you. But better devastation and embarrassment than damnation. You want him on his feet and forgiven before the Master on the Day of Judgment" (1 Cor. 5:3–5, THE MESSAGE).

Amen.

Chapter 7

HEALING THE WOUNDS OF BETRAYAL

CHARLES SCHULZ, CREATOR of the long-running comic strip *Peanuts*, had a classic illustration of betrayal. The cartoon first appeared in 1951 and has reappeared almost every year since. In this particular cartoon Lucy Van Pelt offers to hold the football for Charlie Brown to kick. In the original cartoon, Lucy was actually afraid that Charlie Brown would kick her hand, so at the last minute she pulled the football out of the way, causing Charlie Brown to fall and hurt himself.

Every autumn the comic strip reappears, with Lucy promising to hold the football then pulling it away at the last second as Charlie Brown falls. Every year she comes up with a reason for him to trust her, and every year she betrays that trust. She actually criticizes him for trusting her, and yet, every year, he does so again.

Charlie Brown's reaction to Lucy is actually the opposite of the way most people respond to betrayal. When we have been betrayed, the natural tendency is to not trust again. In fact, it is difficult to ever get to the place where we feel it is safe to trust again. We are "gun-shy." A person who is gun-shy is afraid of a loud noise (such as that of a gun) or is markedly distrustful or frightened. It can be frustrating having a family member like this. I know from experience.

My daughter Danielle has a little dog named Leela that is gun-shy. When Leela was young, Danielle would bring her into my bathroom and either give her a bath or clean out her ears. She did not mind the bath, but she hated having her ears cleaned. Whenever Danielle would go into our bathroom to get a cotton swab, Leela would hide under the bed. Leela began to associate that bathroom with an unpleasant experience. It did not matter how sweetly Danielle talked to Leela or how many treats she offered her, Leela would not willingly go into that bathroom. She is gun-shy—or maybe cotton-swab-shy!

Those who have been betrayed often become much like my daughter's gun-shy dog. They associate pain with certain experiences. In essence they say, "Hurt me once, shame on you. Hurt me twice, shame on me. I will not give you another opportunity to hurt me. I will not trust again." They associate trust with betrayal, which is a painful experience, and do not want to repeat the experience. In order to avoid betrayal, they choose not to trust anyone again.

For an animal to get over gun-shyness, it must be retrained. For us to overcome the effects of betrayal, we must also go through emotional retraining and healing.

I remember watching one day as my Judas went out to hang himself. I watched and waited. I did not hand him the rope or point him to the tree. I just watched, and as I did I said in my heart, "I will never let anyone else get that close to me!"

Then the Holy Spirit reminded me that if I used that philosophy to weed out all of the Judases, I would potentially be weeding out ninety-nine or a hundred others who could bring value to my life. For every one Judas I may encounter, there might be another thousand relationships that would be a blessing to me. Yes, I could get hurt, but I had to be willing to take the risk.

Love is risky but your life will get very lonely if you live it with your hand warding people away.

> You're familiar with the old written law, "Love your friend," and its unwritten companion, "Hate your enemy." I'm challenging that. I'm telling you to love your enemies. Let them bring out the best in you, not the worst. When someone gives you a hard time, respond with the energies of prayer, for then you are working out of your true selves, your God-created selves. This is what God does. He gives his best—the sun to warm and the rain to nourish—to everyone, regardless: the good and bad, the nice and nasty. If all you do is love the lovable, do you expect a bonus? Anybody can do that. If you simply say hello to those who greet you, do you expect a medal? Any run-of-the-mill sinner does that.
> —MATTHEW 5:44–47, THE MESSAGE

Physical healing is a very important function of the body. It is a process God has put in our cell structure. When your skin is cut, the body immediately begins the healing process. Blood flow to the wounded area is reduced, and proteins in the blood work with plasma to form a scab while the skin underneath works to regenerate itself. The scab is in place to protect the area from further damage and infection.

If a wound does not heal, steps must be taken to receive special treatment. Sometimes a chronic wound must have the dead skin cut away to promote the growth of new skin. This is called debridement. It may also be necessary for a skin graft or oxygen therapy to be performed in order to treat the wound. When specialized care does not help the wound heal, the next course of action may be amputation. Amputation is done when a part of the body is no longer functioning or to stop the spread of infection.

In the same way that physical healing must occur when there has been a physical injury, emotional and spiritual healing is necessary when there has been an emotional wound. Time is a great healer, but it is not the only solution. God gave us His body, the church, as an instrument of healing. Allowing God to heal us can bring us freedom and victory from the devastating effects of bitterness. We also need healing in order to be all that God has purposed for us to be. Only when we have been through the healing process can we see the benefits of betrayal. (And there are benefits; we will discuss them in chapter 10.)

There are times when we may need to receive special care for the emotional wounds we have suffered. We may need to have some dead tissue cut away. We may need a spiritual skin graft. We must do whatever it takes, because the danger of not receiving healing is amputation.

Satan does not want you to heal so he will try to keep you from seeking specialized care for your wounds. He will isolate you from others so you will walk alone in your pain. This may trigger depression and anger. But no matter how deeply you've been wounded, God has a prescription for your pain.

A Prescription for Healing

While walking through one of my Judas experiences, I asked two godly men to hold me accountable for my attitude. During this time, I read Psalm 37 every day and made it a part of my devotions. When I felt myself becoming angry, cynical, or jaded, I would go back to the Word of God. There were days when I must have read that passage once every hour. The truths in that psalm sustained me in my darkest hours. Let's walk through that passage and see it as a prescription for healing.

Do not fret

In verses 1 and 2 of Psalm 37 the psalmist encourages us to allow nature to take its course. Those who are wicked will not last forever. They will wither and fade away if we allow God to do His work.

> Do not fret because of those who are evil or be envious of those who do wrong; for like the grass they will soon wither, like green plants they will soon die away.
> —PSALM 37:1–2, NIV

In Psalm 103:6 we are told that God will make everything all right. When we are victims, He will put us back on our feet. That is our assurance from God's Word!

Trust God

> Trust in the LORD and do good; dwell in the land and enjoy safe pasture.
> —PSALM 37:3, NIV

When we trust God and live according to His Word, He promises that we will be safe and enjoy our lives. Too many of us forget that we are not put on this earth to just live. We are put here to fellowship with our Father and enjoy our journey to heaven!

Know you are not alone

God promises His presence will be with us (Matt. 28:19–20), that He will not put us in a position that will destroy us (1 Cor. 10:13), and that there is freedom in forgiveness.

The psalmist said:

> Take delight in the LORD, and he will give you the desires of your heart.
> —PSALM 37:4, NIV

When you truly turn your difficulties over to God and leave them in His hands, He will validate your efforts, vindicate you, and bring justice.

> Commit your way to the LORD; trust in him and he will do this: He will make your righteous reward shine like the dawn, your vindication like the noonday sun.
> —PSALM 37:5–6, NIV

Wait on God

We often look at circumstances and become frustrated when it seems that those who have wronged us are having success in their lives. We want God to exact immediate justice, but our timetable is not necessarily God's timetable.

> Be still before the LORD and wait patiently for him; do not fret when people succeed in their ways, when they carry out their wicked schemes.
> —PSALM 37:7, NIV

God is never late, but I admit, it would be nice if He were sometimes early!

Control your temper

Anger does not produce righteousness (James 1:20). Only those who learn self-control and trust will come into full possession of their inheritance.

> Refrain from anger and turn from wrath; do not fret—
> it leads only to evil. For those who are evil will be
> destroyed, but those who hope in the LORD will inherit
> the land.
> —PSALM 37:8–9, NIV

Know that the wicked will not always win

There will come a day when the weapons the wicked use will be turned on them, a day when those who have been wronged will see the vengeance of the Lord. It is better for us to be godly and have little than to be evil and rich, for the strength of the wicked will be shattered, but the Lord takes care of the godly.

> A little while, and the wicked will be no more; though
> you look for them, they will not be found. But the meek
> will inherit the land and enjoy great peace and pros-
> perity. The wicked plot against the righteous and gnash
> their teeth at them; but the Lord laughs at the wicked,
> for he knows their day is coming. The wicked draw the
> sword and bend the bow to bring down the poor and
> needy, to slay those whose ways are upright. But their
> swords will pierce their own hearts, and their bows will
> be broken. Better the little that the righteous have than
> the wealth of many wicked; for the power of the wicked
> will be broken, but the LORD upholds the righteous.
> —PSALM 37:10–17, NIV

Remember that God keeps the records

God knows who is blameless and who is guilty. He knows who has placed themselves in His care and established their dependence on Him. His provision is more than enough, even in times of personal tragedy.

> The blameless spend their days under the LORD's care, and their inheritance will endure forever. In times of disaster they will not wither; in days of famine they will enjoy plenty. But the wicked will perish: Though the LORD's enemies are like the flowers of the field, they will be consumed, they will go up in smoke.
>
> —PSALM 37:18–20, NIV

Be generous and let God bless you

> The wicked borrow and do not repay, but the righteous give generously; those the LORD blesses will inherit the land, but those he curses will be destroyed.
>
> —PSALM 37:21–22, NIV

Trust God to show you what to do

> The LORD makes firm the steps of the one who delights in him; though he may stumble, he will not fall, for the LORD upholds him with his hand.
>
> —PSALM 37:23–24, NIV

Believe that God will not abandon you and your children

You will remain safe and protected from evil:

> I was young and now I am old, yet I have never seen the righteous forsaken or their children begging bread. They

are always generous and lend freely; their children will be a blessing. Turn from evil and do good; then you will dwell in the land forever. For the LORD loves the just and will not forsake his faithful ones.

—PSALM 37:25–28, NIV

Trust that God will vindicate and rescue you

Those who are godly offer good counsel; they teach right from wrong. They have made God's law their own so they will never slip from His path. The wicked wait in ambush for the godly, looking for an excuse to kill them. But the Lord will not let the wicked succeed or let the godly be condemned when they are put on trial. Your only hope is in the Lord. If you travel steadily along His path, He will honor you. You will see the wicked destroyed.

> The righteous will inherit the land and dwell in it forever. The mouths of the righteous utter wisdom, and their tongues speak what is just. The law of their God is in their hearts; their feet do not slip. The wicked lie in wait for the righteous, intent on putting them to death; but the LORD will not leave them in the power of the wicked or let them be condemned when brought to trial. Hope in the LORD and keep his way. He will exalt you to inherit the land; when the wicked are destroyed, you will see it.
>
> I have seen a wicked and ruthless man flourishing like a luxuriant native tree, but he soon passed away and was no more; though I looked for him, he could not be found. Consider the blameless, observe the upright; a future awaits those who seek peace. But all sinners will be destroyed; there will be no future for the wicked. The salvation of the righteous comes from the LORD; he is their stronghold in time of trouble. The LORD helps them

and delivers them; he delivers them from the wicked and saves them, because they take refuge in him.

—PSALM 37:29–40, NIV

The Word of God is alive. It is water to the thirsty and bread to the hungry. It is balm for the broken and for the hurting soul. When you read the words of the psalmist David, you will see that he was a hurting soul who found sustenance in his relationship with the Father. These twelve principles will empower you to walk through betrayal without becoming bitter. Allow Psalm 37 to bring new life to you as you practice its principles. I encourage you to read it again and again in its entirety and make it a prayer:

> Fret not yourself because of evildoers, neither be envious against those who work unrighteousness (that which is not upright or in right standing with God).
>
> For they shall soon be cut down like the grass, and wither as the green herb.
>
> Trust (lean on, rely on, and be confident) in the Lord and do good; so shall you dwell in the land and feed surely on His faithfulness, and truly you shall be fed.
>
> Delight yourself also in the Lord, and He will give you the desires and secret petitions of your heart.
>
> Commit your way to the Lord [roll and repose each care of your load on Him]; trust (lean on, rely on, and be confident) also in Him and He will bring it to pass.
>
> And He will make your uprightness and right standing with God go forth as the light, and your justice and right as [the shining sun of] the noonday.
>
> Be still and rest in the Lord; wait for Him and patiently lean yourself upon Him; fret not yourself because of him who prospers in his way, because of the man who brings wicked devices to pass.

Cease from anger and forsake wrath; fret not yourself—it tends only to evildoing.

For evildoers shall be cut off, but those who wait and hope and look for the Lord [in the end] shall inherit the earth.

For yet a little while, and the evildoers will be no more; though you look with care where they used to be, they will not be found.

But the meek [in the end] shall inherit the earth and shall delight themselves in the abundance of peace.

The wicked plot against the [uncompromisingly] righteous (the upright in right standing with God); they gnash at them with their teeth.

The Lord laughs at [the wicked], for He sees that their own day [of defeat] is coming.

The wicked draw the sword and bend their bows to cast down the poor and needy, to slay those who walk uprightly (blameless in conduct and in conversation).

The swords [of the wicked] shall enter their own hearts, and their bows shall be broken.

Better is the little that the [uncompromisingly] righteous have than the abundance [of possessions] of many who are wrong and wicked.

For the arms of the wicked shall be broken, but the Lord upholds the [consistently] righteous.

The Lord knows the days of the upright and blameless, and their heritage will abide forever.

They shall not be put to shame in the time of evil; and in the days of famine they shall be satisfied.

But the wicked shall perish, and the enemies of the Lord shall be as the fat of lambs [that is consumed in smoke] and as the glory of the pastures. They shall vanish; like smoke shall they consume away.

The wicked borrow and pay not again [for they may

be unable], but the [uncompromisingly] righteous deal kindly and give [for they are able].

For such as are blessed of God shall [in the end] inherit the earth, but they that are cursed of Him shall be cut off.

The steps of a [good] man are directed and established by the Lord when He delights in his way [and He busies Himself with his every step].

Though he falls, he shall not be utterly cast down, for the Lord grasps his hand in support and upholds him.

I have been young and now am old, yet have I not seen the [uncompromisingly] righteous forsaken or their seed begging bread.

All day long they are merciful and deal graciously; they lend, and their offspring are blessed.

Depart from evil and do good; and you will dwell forever [securely].

For the Lord delights in justice and forsakes not His saints; they are preserved forever, but the offspring of the wicked [in time] shall be cut off.

[Then] the [consistently] righteous shall inherit the land and dwell upon it forever.

The mouth of the [uncompromisingly] righteous utters wisdom, and his tongue speaks with justice.

The law of his God is in his heart; none of his steps shall slide.

The wicked lie in wait for the [uncompromisingly] righteous and seek to put them to death.

The Lord will not leave them in their hands, or [suffer them to] condemn them when they are judged.

Wait for and expect the Lord and keep and heed His way, and He will exalt you to inherit the land; [in the end] when the wicked are cut off, you shall see it.

I have seen a wicked man in great power and spreading himself like a green tree in its native soil,

Yet he passed away, and behold, he was not; yes, I sought and inquired for him, but he could not be found.

Mark the blameless man and behold the upright, for there is a happy end for the man of peace.

As for transgressors, they shall be destroyed together; in the end the wicked shall be cut off.

But the salvation of the [consistently] righteous is of the Lord; He is their Refuge and secure Stronghold in the time of trouble.

And the Lord helps them and delivers them; He delivers them from the wicked and saves them, because they trust and take refuge in Him.

—PSALM 37, AMP

The Word of God can bring healing to your heart, mind, and spirit if you meditate on its truth and allow it to perform its work.

Chapter 8

LEADING THROUGH BETRAYAL

WHEN JELLY AND I moved to our current pastorate, we inherited a small pastoral staff. The church had a long history and within that history was immorality. In fact, even one of the early pastors had a moral failure. This history contributed to attitudes of distrust in the church.

I immediately began to put boundaries in place to help protect both myself and the staff from any indiscretions or any hint of immorality. Office doors were left open when someone of the opposite sex was present. Staff members could not have lunch alone with a person of the opposite sex unless that person was his or her spouse. Spouses were required to be a vital part of the staff member's ministry. Assistants created weekly agendas that were to be strictly followed. I truly thought we had put enough hedges in place to protect the pastors and their families. I was wrong.

If someone wants to commit immorality, it does not matter how many roadblocks are put in the way, he will find a path to his destruction. Within ten months of my arrival one of my staff members betrayed the church body by having an affair with someone on the support staff. When the affair was confirmed, I had to make a choice. I could sweep it under the rug and never let anyone know about it. I could allow the staff member to resign quietly and seek a position in another church in another town. But as I said previously, if you leave a church wrong you will arrive at the new church wrong. If I allowed this to happen, I would simply pass on the betrayal to another unsuspecting body of believers. By doing so, I would then become a part of the betrayal.

My other choice was to follow the biblical pattern of discipline and restoration outlined in Galatians 6:1–3: "Brothers and sisters, if someone is caught in a sin, you who live by the Spirit should restore that person gently. But watch yourself, or you also may be tempted. Carry each other's burdens, and in this way you will fulfill the law of Christ. If anyone thinks they are something when they are not, they deceive themsevles" (NIV).

I could expose the affair and deal with the fallout, which would give this person a chance to be truly restored and not to merely move on. I chose to expose the affair and implement the disciplinary process for our particular organization. This person went into a two-year restoration process during which he and his wife stepped out of ministry, received counseling, and worked on their marriage. I knew their marriage had to be sound before their ministry could reach the level God intended for them. I realize that we live in a day and time when it is not popular to confront sin. But as the church we are ambassadors of another kingdom. We are not called to conform to culture but to challenge it with the truth of God's Word.

When I first learned about the affair, I felt I had failed the church, the official board, and the people directly involved in this individual's ministry. I knew there would be a lot of pain and heartache associated with his leaving. I did not want to see people hurting because of the actions of one of my staff members. I thought I should have seen this coming. I thought I should have been able to intervene before an inappropriate relationship escalated into an affair.

While these individuals were involved in the affair, the church was experiencing one of the greatest times of growth it had seen up to that point. God was moving. People were coming to Christ. The church had almost doubled in size and appeared to be healthy. How could such good and such bad be happening at the same time?

Even healthy organizations are confronted with betrayal. Anyone can encounter a Judas. If someone chooses to betray someone else, that is no reason to believe an entire organization is failing. Nor does it mean that everyone is a Judas. It simply means that one person was weak and allowed Satan to use him to try to bring destruction to the leader and the organization.

Fortunately I soon realized that I did not have to feel guilty for not recognizing the betrayal more quickly. I worked with the staff member who failed morally every day. We ate lunch together, went to funerals together, led church services together, and prayed together. Our children even spent time together. Still, I did not see the betrayal until it was too late.

In chapter 6 I wrote about my first Judas in ministry. I remember thinking that I had failed God and the organization I was leading because I allowed the one who betrayed me to be in authority. I had promoted the person's abilities and not his character. I had no idea that a Judas spirit was lurking beneath the surface and had seized the opportunity to gain control. At that time I was disappointed in myself and criticized many decisions

I made. I felt so guilty, and I allowed the enemy to really beat me up emotionally. Satan is the accuser of the brethren, and when you are down, he will use any and everything to beat you up. Not every thought is from God, even ones that may seem noble. Satan was feeding my self-recrimination and using it against me!

I was praying one day and repenting again for what I thought was my failure in the situation, and God told me to stop asking for forgiveness. I knew I was hearing the voice of God in my heart. He started taking me through Scripture, showing me that I had already done what I was supposed to do. First John 1:9 says, "If we confess our sins, he is faithful and just to forgive us our sins, and to cleanse us from all unrighteousness" (KJV).

I had already asked for forgiveness. By bringing it up again and again, I was saying in essence that His blood was not enough to cover that sin. The Holy Spirit reminded me that I was a new creature in Christ and that old things had passed away:

> Therefore, if anyone is in Christ, he is a new creation; old things have passed away; behold, all things have become new.
> —2 CORINTHIANS 5:17

He reminded me that there was no condemnation in Him:

> There is therefore now no condemnation to those who are in Christ Jesus, who do not walk according to the flesh, but according to the Spirit.
> —ROMANS 8:1

Even after the Lord reminded me of these truths, I still felt guilty for not seeing my betrayer. Thankfully the Holy Spirit again spoke into my heart and told me that the reason I did not see the betrayer was because my heart was pure before Him. I had been looking for the good in people, not the bad. That was what I was called to do: to see the good in others. People need someone who can see the good in them, not the bad. They need someone to believe in them.

Have you ever heard the truism, "It takes one to know one"? It applies here. Only deceivers can pick up deception quickly. They know one another because they have the same spirits. The exception for this rule of thumb is when a person has a spiritual gift of knowledge or discerning of spirits. Realizing that I was only doing what God designed me to do released me from the condemnation and guilt.

You may have done the same thing I did. You may have held yourself accountable for betrayals that occurred under your watch. How many wives blame themselves for a husband who strays? How many children blame themselves for a parent who leaves? How many pastors blame themselves, as I did, for a member or staffer who betrays the church? They pronounce themselves guilty, thinking they should have seen this or that. No! We are to see the good in people before the evil. To do otherwise is unhealthy.

If you were deceived in the past and are still blaming yourself for the pain caused to you, your family, or your organization, it is time to stop allowing the enemy to ruin your life. Neither you nor your organization failed because you encountered a Judas. Betrayal is one of Satan's favorite strategies; it is what led to his fall from heaven.

When you start looking for a Judas in everyone you meet, you become a cynic. We already have too many cynics in the church. We need shepherds. Shepherds die for their sheep, even when their sheep do foolish things.

Beating yourself up does no good to restore health to a church or organization after betrayal. But there are some practical steps leaders can take to recover and possibly bring restoration when betrayal has occurred.

Let Your Judas Expose Himself

A martyr is someone who chooses to die rather than deny a strongly held belief, especially a religious belief. A Judas is more interested in being right than in the health or success of the organization he is supposed to be serving. He is willing to make sacrifices or suffer greatly to advance his influence. If you make a martyr out of a Judas instead of allowing him to be exposed for what he is, people in the organization will become confused and may align themselves with him, thus creating division. Don't give your betrayer the opportunity to build an alliance against you. It will take every ounce of restraint on your part, but it will be worth it.

I once served on the board of directors of a prestigious university. During a leadership training session, the board president told us, "Never waste a good hanging." By that he meant that if you had to fire someone do it in such a way that others in leadership would not make the same mistake. That philosophy will not apply to a Judas. When Judas Iscariot went out and hanged himself, he declared his own guilt and Jesus's innocence. That is why it is important for us to be sensitive to the leadership of the Holy Spirit when dealing with someone who betrays us.

A Judas can hide behind the cloak of religion only for so long. The idea is to allow them to expose themselves. There is a rule of thumb in leadership that we sometimes forget: as long as the leader is the only one in pain, you withstand the pain until you can remove the problem with the least amount of damage to the organization. When the pain that leader is feeling becomes the pain of the organization, you move quickly. As a leader you must endure the pain of the betrayal. If the betrayer begins to impact the organization, take steps to minimize his influence. But don't seek to expose him; he will do that himself.

Don't Be Rash

A Judas is usually something of a bully. A bully is habitually cruel or overbearing, especially to weaker or less influential people. He will not listen to reason. He will try to run over you. He will try to tell you how to handle things in the organization and in the process of changing policy he will give himself more power. He will argue with you, publicly if he feels it is necessary. He will threaten you.

I do not function well when I am threatened. I react; most men do. When I was a child and even into my young adult years, my first reaction to a threat was to hit the person who was threatening me. Some people argue; some walk away; some push the other person away emotionally; some people get physical. Our reactions are often based upon our personalities, our personal history, and where we are in our walk with God, but everyone responds in some way to threats. When you are a leader, your reaction will make matters either worse or better.

When someone threatens us, our bodies and minds begin to employ a defense mechanism. This is something we use subconsciously to protect ourselves against anxiety or things that cause anxiety.

Have you ever been sucker punched? A sucker punch is a blow that comes without warning. The person who is hit has no time to prepare or defend himself. In other words, he doesn't see it coming. After it happens once, you will likely get defensive whenever someone gets a little aggressive with you so you won't be sucker punched again.

I once had an individual try to intimidate me. I knew it would not take much strength to lay him out on the floor. I was already frustrated and started trying to justify my intended action with scripture: "Whatever your hand finds to do, do it with your might" (Eccles. 9:10).

Then the Holy Spirit spoke into my spirit and said, "I died for him too."

I thought, "Yeah, right."

Then He again spoke, "Yes, I did. I died for him too."

When I was a student at Southeastern University, I had a professor named Crandall Miller. At the beginning and the end of every class, Professor Miller would say, "What you feed grows; what you starve dies. What you feed grows; what you starve dies."

As I stood before that bully who was trying to intimidate me, Professor Miller's words came into my mind, "What you feed grows; what you starve dies." It felt like the spirit of God was saying to me, "You pop him in the mouth like you want to do, and you will feed your flesh. You will feed that flesh and make it harder for us to keep your flesh under control." Convicted by the Holy Spirit, I let out my breath and opened my fist. I did not hit him, even though I still wanted to!

Our carnality is tested when we encounter a Judas. A Judas wants you to operate on the same fleshly level as he does. Stand your ground but do it with the grace the Lord intends. Don't let him bully your family; don't let him bully you. Stand your ground. You can speak to the person trying to bully you and say, "You will not do this." You can take a stand without being unkind and having your words full of venom. It takes a lot of work and submission to the Holy Spirit to do this, but you can do it.

Don't Lash Out

At some point in time, after a Judas is rebuked, he will go too far. He will say or do something that others see and be judged wrong in his actions. Let him do it; it is his decision. The Bible says that Judas threw the money on the floor at the feet of the Sanhedrin and went out and hanged himself. He did it himself. He did not need Peter, James, John, or anyone else to assist him.

You do not have to buy Judas the rope or lead him to the tree. You may want to hand the rope to him as he is standing under the tree but resist the urge. He will do this himself because he is a betrayer.

It is very difficult not to strike out and hurt someone emotionally, verbally, or any other way when you are betrayed. Opportunities will arise for you to strike back, but how you behave when those opportunities arise will determine whether you fulfill the destiny of God for your life.

No matter what has happened in your life, the Spirit of God still wants to do great things for and with you. You may think your life is too troubled, confused, or embarrassing for God to be interested in you, but that is not true. God has a specific purpose for your life. Betrayal in and of itself will not derail that destiny but how you respond to betrayal can.

In 1 Samuel 24 we find David hiding from Saul in a cave. Saul was jealous of David and wanted to kill him; he had tried to do so more than once. In this passage Saul comes into the recesses of the cave to relieve himself. While Saul was in there taking care of business, Joab and Abaci told David, "This is the day of which the LORD said to you, 'Behold, I will deliver your enemy into your hand, that you may do to him as it seems good to you'" (v. 4).

In essence, they were saying, "Let us rise up and kill him."

David said, "No, I will not do it." But David did rise up and cut off a piece of Saul's robe without his knowing it. David had been close enough to kill him if he had chosen to do so.

The kings of that day wore tassels on their robes representing the Word of God. Kings were keepers of the Word, and they were to walk according to the Torah. What this great story in 1 Samuel 24 is telling us is that you have to learn how to behave in a cave before you can rule a kingdom.

When David cut off that piece of Saul's robe, he was telling Saul: "You are violating the Word of God by the way you are treating me."

But David knew how he was supposed to conduct himself, and he knew that by cutting a piece of Saul's robe, he had not conducted himself in a manner that was pleasing to God. God will never promote you to your destiny and into His will if you don't learn decorum. You may find yourself in places you never thought you would be, facing things you never thought you would face, but the way you behave in your cave will determine what God can do for you.

Saul walked into a cave where David's entire army was hidden. At that moment David could have put an end to the war between him and Saul. Yet he chose to not end Saul's life, to not put his hand against the anointed king. Still, David's decision to cut a piece of Saul's robe left him very remorseful (v. 5).

When David held up the edge of the robe, both David and Saul's armies saw a man who was repenting for his actions.

David proclaimed that the Lord would be judge between the two of them. God can bless those who walk in humility.

One of the reasons God loved David so much was that David respected the anointing of God and those He had anointed. David walked in humility before God. He remained faithful to God even when things were difficult. How you behave in your cave will determine your destiny. It will determine whether you ever make it out of the cave.

Watch Your Attitude

There was once a family of betrayers attending the church of a friend. My friend knew he had to keep his spirit right before God or the church would suffer. To help him do that, he asked two very godly men in the church to help him walk circumspectly. He gave them permission to hold him accountable if they saw anything in his life that would be displeasing to his heavenly Father.

This was a crucial time in his life when he needed strong accountability. These two men did as he asked. There were times when he wanted to confront this family and have a physical altercation, but the two men in the church helped him keep his attitude correct.

There are times in life when we all need to be held in accountability. In the Gospel of Luke Jesus told His disciples that He not only knew who would betray Him but also that He had chosen that very person to walk with Him in a close relationship.

> "But there are some of you who do not believe." For Jesus knew from the beginning who they were who did not believe, and who would betray Him. And He said, "Therefore I have said to you that no one can come to Me

unless it has been granted to him by My Father." From that time many of His disciples went back and walked with Him no more. Then Jesus said to the twelve, "Do you also want to go away?" But Simon Peter answered Him, "Lord, to whom shall we go? You have the words of eternal life. Also we have come to believe and know that You are the Christ, the Son of the living God." Jesus answered them, "Did I not choose you, the twelve, and one of you is a devil?" He spoke of Judas Iscariot, the son of Simon, for it was he who would betray Him, being one of the twelve.

—JOHN 6:64–71

Jesus told the disciples that He knew what would happen; He already knew someone would betray Him, and He knew exactly who that person was.

There have been Judases in various organizations I have led. I have known certain individuals were "shooting" at me. Even in these kinds of situations you must show grace and love, which is very difficult. Anyone can love a person who is nice to him, but the real test comes when you must love someone who is unkind to you. There are people who appear to not love anyone. They seem to be mad at the world. Although you try, there is nothing you or anyone else can do to please them. At some point they turn on you and you have a decision to make: you can either react to their words and actions or do as Jesus told us to do. He said, "Love your enemies…and pray for those who spitefully use you" (Matt. 5:44). Love your Judases. When you can do that, the love of God is in you.

The love of God makes you different. There were times when the only thing that kept me from being destroyed by Judases was the fact that I was different from them. I did not respond the way they did. The fact that I did not act like them drew such

change how you relate to people and how you treat people. If a Judas hurts you so deeply that you say, "I don't want to be close to anybody," then he has won. He will let you sit in church. He will let you pay your tithes. He will even let you teach a Sunday school class. He does not care if you continue to work in the church or in ministry, because you have limited what God can do with your life when you choose to not love others. You will in some ways share your hurt with others and poison the body. That is what Satan desires.

I have had about five Judases in my life. After the first one I wanted out of the ministry. I was still planning to serve Jesus and go to church. I just wanted no more to do with church people. I remember telling Jelly that I did not want to continue in ministry, that I was finished. We had completed our new sanctuary, and I was emotionally, physically, and spiritually exhausted. Then Judas showed up.

I left our town to visit my parents in Charleston, South Carolina, for a few days. I took our five-year-old daughter, Jordan, with me. When I arrived at my mother's house, she told me that she was leaving for revival service and that I needed to come too. I was in no mood to go to church. I'd had all I wanted of church people.

While I was sitting by her pool and contemplating what kind of secular job I could get, the Holy Spirit started dealing with me. I was a pastor who had told people they needed to run to Jesus whenever they had a problem. But when I had a problem, I was sitting down, pouting, and daring God to do anything in my life. I was like the prophet Elijah, who went into a cave to hide. Just as Elijah had done, I told God all the things I had done and how my Judas was attacking me, my credibility, and my family.

So he said, "I have been very zealous for the LORD God of hosts; for the children of Israel have forsaken

Your covenant, torn down Your altars, and killed Your prophets with the sword. I alone am left; and they seek to take my life."

—1 Kings 19:10

Just as He had a mandate for Elijah, God had a mandate for me. I did not know when or how He would deliver it, but I knew God had a word for me and that I needed to be in church that night. A visiting evangelist preached that night, but I do not remember a thing he said. When he gave the altar call, four hundred to five hundred people responded, including me.

Even though I knew I needed to be there, I had a really bad attitude. I told God, "OK, I'm here. If You want to touch me, fine. If not, I'm done." Nothing happened. I went back to my seat and sat down and put my head in my hands. All of a sudden something in my spirit was released. I remember weeping uncontrollably. About that time the evangelist came back to where I was sitting and laid his hand on me. I remember getting mad at my mother because I thought she had told him about me and that she sent him over to me.

Then I saw my mother on the other side of the church; she didn't even know what he was doing. The evangelist started giving me a word of knowledge and prophesying over me. He didn't know me and had not been sent by my mother. When he began speaking, he was very direct and specific. He spoke in detail about things that I had not even told my wife. I did not want her to know the hurtful things that were in my heart. I knew she did not need to hear those things so I kept them between me and God.

After the evangelist spoke the words of knowledge over my life, he began to prophesy. I did not know that the things he was prophesying would occur fifteen to twenty years down the road, but I knew that there was truth in what he spoke. Those words broke the dam of hurt in my heart, and I knew I had to make a choice: Would I choose to continue to love and minister to people even though I would probably have another Judas come into my life?

That day I decided not to let one, two, three, or ten people change the way I lived my life or served the Lord. And healing came to me. Whenever I encounter one of the former Judases I am able to embrace them and tell them I love and pray for them and really mean it. It took an act of God, but the transformation in my heart finally happened. I was able to forgive.

When you have been betrayed, Satan wants to change how you react to people. You may have been betrayed by your children. You may have been betrayed by your parents. You may have been betrayed by a spouse. Whatever the situation is, God does not want you to say you will never get close to anyone again.

Jesus wants us to keep loving others. That is what He does for us when we betray Him by willfully sinning against Him. Even in our sinfulness Jesus keeps loving us, reaching out to us, and caring for us.

What will you do with your Judas? I am never going on vacation with my Judas. I am not telling you to buddy up with those who have betrayed you. I am encouraging you not to hold other people at arm's length because of what one or two or five or ten people have done to you. Allow God's grace to manifest in your life.

If you want healing, if you want to love and trust others, if you want to have healthy relationships, you can. Good things can happen in your life if you choose to keep loving people despite the hurt and betrayal. The choice is yours.

Chapter 9

SATAN'S ENDGAME

T HE BIBLE SAYS, "And we know that all things work together for good to those who love God, to those who are the called according to His purpose" (Rom. 8:28). We often recite verses like this one, knowing they are true in our heads but not believing them in our hearts. When we walk through difficult times, it is hard to imagine how in the world God could possibly cause them to work for good in our lives. That is because we look at the individual events of life while God looks at the whole of our lives. God has a panoramic view of our past, present, and future. He is omniscient, so He sees it all.

Consider the same passage as written in THE MESSAGE:

> Meanwhile, the moment we get tired in the waiting, God's Spirit is right alongside helping us along. If we don't know how or what to pray, it doesn't matter. He does our praying in and for us, making prayer out of our wordless sighs, our aching groans. He knows us far better than we know ourselves, knows our pregnant

condition, and keeps us present before God. That's why we can be so sure that every detail in our lives of love for God is worked into something good.

—Romans 8:26–28

God does work every detail of our lives into something good. That certainly does not mean He sends only good things our way. Nor does it mean that He sends evil our way to help us grow spiritually. It means that when bad things happen, God can use them as learning experiences and make them into something good for our lives.

Satan is the one who brings evil into our lives, not God. In order to reduce his power in our lives, we must understand Satan's plan and purpose for bringing us pain and heartache. The enemy is not omniscient, but he does have an agenda: our destruction. Satan will use any tool available to him to destroy us, but betrayal is one of his favorites.

Many years ago I met a man who was an children's pastor at a church and was also pursuing a bachelor's degree in elementary education. While in college he had developed the church's children's ministry and oversaw the Royal Rangers, a ministry for boys that is similar to Boy Scouts. Due to his hard work and passion for what he was doing, he was offered a position as a part-time pastor. Later that year his wife was offered a position as the pastor's personal assistant.

Both he and his wife accepted the positions they had been offered. While he was in college, they had endured some very difficult times, both financially and emotionally. They had two daughters, but they also suffered miscarriages and a baby was stillborn, all of which had taken an emotional toll on both of them. These new opportunities seemed to be a welcome reprieve from the hardship they had faced.

This couple had been on staff for a few years when they began to have some trouble in their home. One day she walked into the pastor's office, resigned as his assistant, and left her husband. Upon hearing of the dilemma in their home, I went to offer my counsel and tried to help save the marriage. The more I counseled, the more I knew I was failing. She had decided she was leaving and nothing would change her mind. It takes two willing people for a marriage to work. If one of those people does not want to save the marriage, it is doomed for failure.

Not long after his wife resigned, the children's pastor went into his senior pastor's office to resign his position as well. When I asked him why he had done this, he told me that since his wife was divorcing him, he knew he could not stay. I knew he had done nothing wrong, so I tried to encourage him to remain on staff. He wept as I spoke with him and told me that all he wanted to do was to be an ordained minister. Now his dreams were destroyed.

I reminded him that when God called him, God knew what was going to happen to his marriage. Even though God knew this young man's marriage would end, He still had called him to be a minister. Somehow God was going to work this marital situation for his good.

Life went on for him and his two little girls, of whom he had custody, but it was very difficult. Still, he kept his faith and continued to serve the Lord. About two years after the divorce, he and his high school friend reconnected. When he asked my opinion on whether he should begin dating her, I encouraged him to proceed with the relationship.

In time the two married, blended their families together, and moved to Florida. He went on to earn a master's degree and began teaching elementary school in Florida. This young man had always been very creative, and he took that creativity into the classroom. He did such a phenomenal job that his school nominated him Teacher of the Year. Then after earning that honor, he was named Teacher of the Year for his entire county. When he called to tell me what God was doing in his life, he had been nominated Teacher of the Year for the state of Florida.

He received that honor as well. As Florida's Teacher of the Year he was able to travel around the state with the governor and lead education-related events. During this time, he was also working to complete his doctorate. As is the case with most dissertations, the writing and researching process proved to be rigorous and difficult. He asked me to pray for him over those next few months as he traveled and completed his dissertation.

I was honored to do so, and we stayed in close contact during that time. One day he again called and told me that he was on his way to Dallas for a national Teacher of the Year event. He was one of the top four finalists out of four million teachers in America.

He later went on to become the dean of education at a respected Christian university. Years earlier when he walked through a divorce, he couldn't see how God could use him again. He was broken by betrayal and devastated by the turn his life was taking. Yet God caused all things to work together for his good. One decision after another God led him straight into the destiny He had planned for him all along. It took twenty years for the "good" to become evident, but the Lord worked everything together for this young man's benefit and for the good of the kingdom.

You may be going through some things you don't really understand right now, but know this: God can make things right. God can use what you've been going through for good. He will turn it around—if you choose to get better and not bitter.

My friend kept pursuing God and His will for his life. He lost almost everything after his divorce, but he persevered even when things looked the worst. He kept his heart pure before God, and God used the bad circumstances to show my friend that all things do indeed work together for the good of those who love the Lord and are called according to His purpose. In addition to all the good he does in the field of education, he also has used his testimony to help heal hearts that have been broken through betrayal.

David has a similar story. He came into my office as a hurting, broken young man. He had been through a bitter divorce and had almost lost all hope of having a relationship with his daughter. He made a commitment to the Lord and began to set new priorities in his life. He had to make some tough stands, but he surrendered his plans to the Lord and allowed God to direct him. In time God brought a beautiful woman into David's life. They married and had a child together. The daughter that he thought was lost to him eventually moved in with him and his new family. She finished high school and college and is now married to a pastor. David now mentors people who have been through heartache similar to what he endured. He has been able to use the very negativity the enemy thought would destroy his life to help others heal.

Satan Wants to Destroy Your Future

In a war one of the most important things to do is to anticipate the plans of the enemy. The troops need to know whether the enemy is going to attack on land or sea or from the air; they need to know when, where, and how to engage their enemy. Once they know the plans, they can be fully armed and ready to face the battle. Spiritual warfare is similar. When you know Satan's plans, and when, where, and how he is going to attack, you can be prepared to fight a good fight.

We read in John 10:10, "The thief does not come except to steal, and to kill, and to destroy. I have come that they may have life, and that they may have it more abundantly." Satan always has the same goal: he wants to kill, steal, and destroy. If we want to win against Satan, we have to realize that he wants to destroy us. He doesn't just want us to have a bad day or to lose an account; he wants us to miss everything God has for us. He doesn't want us to play our role in God's kingdom agenda. Satan does not come haphazardly into our lives. He looks for a way to bring the most pain and hurt, and few things are more devastating than betrayal. Realizing Satan's endgame is key to winning in spiritual warfare.

Satan uses betrayal to steal our joy. There is nothing that can wound your soul and heart more than betrayal. Betrayal is so painful it can cause us to focus more on the betrayal and the betrayer than on God. With our focus no longer on the Lord, we may begin to listen to the lies the enemy whispers into our hearts: "I am ruined." "My credibility is gone." "I will lose everything." Those lies will burrow deeper and deeper into our hearts until they become truth to us, even though they have been whispered into our spirits by the father of lies (John 8:44). As we believe the lies, our joy slowly melts away and is replaced by despair.

I had been a pastor for two years when a man came into my office for counseling and told me it would have been easier for him to bury his wife than to see her holding the arm of another man. Roger was a good man, but he didn't turn to the Lord until his wife, who was a member of our church, told him she was leaving. He accepted Christ, but their marriage still ended in divorce. Ironically his wife left the church, but he remained and grew in the Lord. I came to respect him. He was a man's man who grieved the loss of his marriage deeply. He wondered if he would ever find joy again. I am happy to say that he did find the joy he longed for and died a happy man because he learned to stop focusing on his wife and turn his attention instead to Christ.

You can have joy during your most difficult time if you will stop focusing on the person who wronged you, what they did, and what you could have done differently. Instead of focusing on what you have lost, focus on what you hope to gain through the experience. Cultivate a spirit of gratitude by reminding yourself of what God has done for you in the past and where He has brought you from.

In recognizing the tactics of the enemy, we must also realize that Satan does not want to merely affect our lives in the present; he wants to destroy our future. If he can change your attitude, he can derail your destiny. Bitter, hurting people produce bitter, hurting people. Healthy people produce healthy people. Your relationships will be affected by betrayal; you will either learn and grow from the experience, or you will let it destroy you.

Have you been around someone who is so negative the atmosphere seems to change when they walk into a room? That is what the enemy wants. When you experience betrayal or any kind of difficulty in life, he wants to breathe anger and hopelessness into your spirit so you will release only anger, bitterness, negativity, or whatever else it takes to destroy you.

Believe Romans 8:28. All things work together for good to them that love the Lord and are called according to His purpose. That does not mean God brought the divorce into the life of my friend. But in His mercy and grace God had already prepared a way to turn the tragedy around for my friend's good—and the good of those he is now able to mentor.

Don't Submit to Satan's Process

Along with the tools Satan uses—namely betrayal, which is intended to steal our joy and derail our destiny—he also has a process that he wants us to walk through. If we submit to Satan's process, our destruction is sure. If, however, we do not submit to his process, our victory is assured!

Fortunately God has given us a prescription to guard against the devil's process. It is found in 1 Peter 5:6–8:

> Therefore humble yourselves under the mighty hand of God, that He may exalt you in due time, casting all your care upon Him, for He cares for you. Be sober, be vigilant; because your adversary the devil walks about like a roaring lion, seeking whom he may devour.

Satan's process is the opposite of what is outlined in this verse. If you want to overcome Satan:

Be humble and resist pride

First Peter 5:6 says to humble yourself! God said, "If you will do that, I'll take care of you." Humility is meekness. Meekness is not weakness. It is controlled strength. Jesus could have destroyed Judas and everyone who came to arrest Him, but He controlled His strength and obeyed the will of the Father. That is what we are to do. We are to obey God's Word as we walk through difficulty. When you humble yourself and walk in meekness, God can lift you up.

Don't carry your cares

We are supposed to cast all our cares upon the Lord (v. 7). The verse is not saying we should lay our cares down gently at the Lord's feet; we are to hurl them away. We are to give the cares away and no longer hold on to them. To put it another way, the cares should no longer be in your possession. The connotation in the verse is that you are to walk away.

The other option is to put the cares on your own shoulders— take them to bed with you, dream about them, pick them up in the morning, walk around with them, take them with you into restaurants and family gatherings, and let the burden of them show on your face. You can even give them a seat of honor in your life. But the Bible says if you carry your cares everywhere you go you will be destroyed by the powers of darkness.

I have a friend who invited me to go surf fishing with him. I told him if our visits to the beach ever coincided, I would be glad to go with him. One such occasion arose when my wife and I were vacationing near the Gulf of Mexico, and I agreed to go with him.

I had never done any surf fishing, but I thought between eight and eleven in the morning would be an ideal time to head to the beach. I figured we'd throw a pole in the water and surf fish. Was I ever wrong! That is not how you surf fish. To surf fish, you have to be out in the water very early. According to my friend, 5:30 in the morning is the best time. Seeing that I had reservations about getting up so early during a vacation, he enticed me with the promise of bacon and eggs before we both headed down to the beach with his son and two sons-in-law.

After breakfast we walked to the beach. The conditions were choppy and the water was moving really fast. The Gulf is usually fairly placid but when the water is choppy, it's pretty rough. I could tell just by the strength of the waves that there were going to be some pretty bad rip tides, but my friend didn't seem at all alarmed. He hooked up a big pole, pulled on the line, and said, "We're going to walk out to the sandbar. It's going to be great!"

I already knew the tide was coming in; on top of that the wind was blowing, and the red flag was flying. The red flag is not there to look pretty; it means stop, don't go, bad. I could tell this was not good, but my friend thought the conditions were great. I knew the sandbar was good only at low tide, but since I knew little about surf fishing, my friend convinced me that he was right.

On our way out to the sandbar the water got deeper and deeper, and the waves were getting rougher. My friend kept moving farther from the shore, saying it was just a little bit farther. All the while I'm thinking we were being pretty stupid. Just as I was thinking that, a wave hit my friend right in the face. He looked at me, bobbing up and down in the water at this point, and conceded that we had better get back to shore. Somehow that shock of water convinced him the conditions were dangerous.

When we got back to shore, we decided to fish from there. We both started casting line in hopes of catching some fish, but every time we cast the line we hauled in eight- and ten-foot-long pieces of seaweed. Every time we cast the line we ended up with more and more seaweed. This was not what I was promised! After we took the seaweed off the lines, my friend suggested we go back to the bay where we could catch some crappie. After fishing for about an hour, all we caught was one four-inch fish that could only be used for bait. At that point I decided I'd had enough.

Some of us give the Lord our cares, but we hold on to the line so we can pull it back when we want, like my friend and I did when we were catching mostly seaweed. What we don't realize is that every time we pull it back toward us, it gets covered with more and more seaweed and debris. We cannot get the seaweed and debris off, so every time we try to cast it away again the load is heavier and more awkward.

The enemy wants us to carry the burden; God doesn't. He wants us to cast our cares on Him and walk away.

Don't be flippant

Let's look again at 1 Peter 5:8:

> Be sober, be vigilant; because your adversary the devil walks about like a roaring lion, seeking whom he may devour.

The Word tells us to be sober and watch out! If you want Satan to destroy your life, do not watch! He will get you.

I have been to Africa twice on big-game hunts. The first time I really didn't want to go. I'd heard the men in my church talk about their hunting trips. They'd get up around four or five o'clock in the morning when it was still dark, go into the woods, sit very quietly, and just wait, wait, wait to see if something came by. That didn't sound like much fun to me, so when someone invited me to go hunting during a visit to Africa, I didn't want to participate. I thought since we were in the Ngorongoro Crater in Tanzania, I would just see the sights from where I was and let the others get up at the crack of dawn to go big-game hunting. I relented only when they told me Tanzania is the best place in the world to go hunting.

That trip taught me that I am truly a big-game hunter at heart. We gathered around 8 a.m. and went to the preserve, where we were met with a table spread out with delicacies that we ate on fine china. After our delicious breakfast we went to the back of the truck we had arrived in and a guide loaded our guns for us and took us where the animals were. They literally put the loaded gun in our hands and told us where to shoot. When we killed an animal, we were posed next to our kill and a guide would take a picture. Then they'd clean the animal and cook it for us. That kind of hunting I liked.

On my hunting trip in Africa I learned that lions sleep about twenty-three hours a day. As long as you find them sleeping, there is no problem. It is when they are awake and walking around that you have a problem. If they are awake and able to move, they are seeking something to devour. They are hungry and they want to eat—*now*.

When a lion is hunting for food, he will look for something that is wounded, young, or outside of the protection of the herd, because those animals make easy prey. Once he has identified his target, he will stalk the animal to separate it from any protection it may be under. Then at just the right moment, he will attack and kill.

Peter said that Satan is like this lion; he walks around seeking something to devour. This is why we must stay sober and remain vigilant. If we are flippant about being faithful and obedient to God and His Word, both of which protect us, we become easy prey.

You Have a Weapon—Use It

Paul admonished us to work out our own salvation with fear and trembling (Phil. 2:12). Knowing what you believe and why you believe it is vitally important when you are in a spiritual battle. If you do not know what you believe, you will fall prey to the enemy's lies. Not knowing what you believe and why you believe it is like walking into a battle with an untried weapon or no weapon at all.

When a soldier goes through basic training, he is given an array of weapons. He is taught what they are and how and when to use them. He learns which ammunition is best and how to load it into the weapon. He learns how to clean the weapon and how to perform other basic maintenance tasks. If he is given a variety of weapons, he must familiarize himself with them all.

He may find one that he prefers, but he must be skilled at using all of them because different battles require different weapons. He may need an M16 for long-distance shooting while a pistol may be sufficient for one-on-one combat. He'll know which weapon is best suited for the battle at hand, and he'll know how to use it.

This is what happens to us when we know what we believe. In Ephesians 6 the Bible lists the armor a spiritual soldier must wear. All of the gear is protective except one item: the sword of the Spirit, which is the Word of God (v. 17). When we know how to use our spiritual weapon, we will be able to defend ourselves against any attack of the enemy, no matter how he strikes. We will know just what to say and do because we know the Word.

When Satan is staring us in the face with his arsenal, we won't have time to go back into basic training to learn our weaponry. When all of hell comes at us with deception and betrayal, we must have our weapon "locked and loaded." We do this by reading and meditating on God's Word. This is what changes the way we think and the way we see our situations. If we do not know what God's Word says, we will be susceptible to anything Satan tells us. When we know the truth—and believe it—we are a serious threat to the enemy.

You Are Not Alone

What you are going through is not unique to you. Sometimes it feels as if no one else could ever have experienced what you are facing. Satan would like you to believe that you are alone and no one could possibly understand what you are going through. But you have brothers and sisters throughout the world who also have experienced the same kind of pain.

Peter wrote:

> Resist him, steadfast in the faith, knowing that the same sufferings are experienced by your brotherhood in the world. But may the God of all grace, who called us to His eternal glory by Christ Jesus, after you have suffered a while, perfect, establish, strengthen, and settle you.
> —1 PETER 5:9–10

This verse tells us that you may suffer a little while, but God will perfect, establish, strengthen, and settle you. The Amplified Bible says that God "will Himself complete and make you what you ought to be, establish and ground you securely, and strengthen, and settle you" (v. 10). He will make you what you ought to be and then He will settle you (solve the problem). That is His promise. God's grace is a wonderful thing.

How do you get through betrayal? You know what Satan wants you to do: he wants you to change the way you look at life and how you look at people. But if you allow the Holy Spirit to do so, He will "establish and ground you securely, and strengthen, and settle you." He will help you keep your heart right before Him, those who have hurt you, and the new people God will bring into your life.

No difficulty you will ever face is unique to you. All over the world brothers and sisters in Christ are facing similar struggles. God will be just as faithful to you as He is to them. If you will be steadfast, God will see you through.

Spiritual pain creates a chasm in the soul that can only be filled with the Holy Spirit. When betrayal creates that chasm, the Holy Spirit will rush in and fill it with Himself. If you have a hole in your heart ten feet deep, you can fill it with anger and bitterness or you can allow the Holy Spirit to rush in and fill it with His presence. Scripture says that in the presence of the Lord, there is fullness of joy (Ps. 16:11). Why not allow the chasm of pain to become a reservoir of joy?

Chapter 10

THE BENEFITS OF BETRAYAL

T HE TITLE OF this chapter must sound like an oxymoron. I once heard someone say betrayal tastes like bile and is about as productive as the dry heaves. If you follow that line of thinking, then you're probably wondering how there could possibly be any benefit in betrayal. I assure you, this chapter's title is not a contradiction in terms. Everything we walk through has benefits. We just have to learn how to see them.

When we are in the thick of the battle, we cannot see who is winning or how we will get to the next front. Because the smoke and gunfire blur our vision, we may not think anyone is left on our side. This is where faith and knowing God's Word come in again. If we really believe Romans 8:28 and are confident that all things work together for the good of them that love the Lord and are called according to His purpose, we will know that God can somehow, someday use the betrayal for our benefit.

Nothing Is Wasted

Everything that comes to us must first go through our heavenly Father. It is "Father filtered." That means nothing comes your way that your heavenly Father has not allowed. What you're facing may not feel like something a loving heavenly Father would allow, but He did and He knows how it will ultimately influence your life for good.

The psalmist wrote:

> But with your own eyes you saw my body being formed.
> Even before I was born, you had written in your book
> everything I would do.
> —PSALM 139:16, CEV

God owns the book that has every day of your life written on its pages. He knows when all the events of your life will take place and how those things will affect your future.

Think about your past. I'm sure there were things you learned in high school that you thought you would never use in life. Maybe you have not used algebra or geometry, but you have certainly worked through complicated problems. Maybe you have never used the material you studied in literature, but you can probably press through and finish reading something you do not enjoy. You may have even learned to read without bias. The rocks, seashells, bugs, and leaves you collected for science projects are probably long forgotten, but you probably remember which glue worked best for each project. There is always a lesson learned. You just have to look for it.

If you have ever been in a car accident caused by your own error, you probably learned to avoid that situation. Our daughter Danielle had just turned sixteen when Jelly sent her to the store to purchase some items she needed for the day. On her way home another sixteen-year-old driver rear-ended her and totaled the car. Danielle suffered whiplash and had to undergo extensive neuromuscular therapy, chiropractic therapy, and physical therapy for six months.

The accident occurred because the other girl was driving with a kitten in the seat beside her. When the kitten jumped off the seat and scurried under her feet, the girl took her eyes off the road for just a moment. That is all it took to cause the accident. The girl learned a very difficult and expensive lesson that day.

There is a television program called *It Only Hurts When I Laugh* that shows clips of people doing foolish things. Of course, the individuals have "epic fails," and we get to laugh at them. One of the funniest videos I've seen is of a girl who stood on a table to look at her shoes and then, it seems, practice her music. Before you know it she has fallen backward off the table. The video has gone viral; at last count it had been viewed by more than 28 million people who now know not to practice singing while standing on a small table.[1]

When our children were growing up, we read fairy tales to them. In every story there was a lesson to be learned: stay away from wolves; don't go into strangers' homes; don't eat candy off anyone's roof; if a goose lays a golden egg it usually belongs to someone else; obey your fairy godmother; and the list goes on. Even as adults there is always a lesson to learn from our experiences. Some lessons slap us in the face and some lessons sneak up on us. We have to look for the lesson; we have to want to learn something positive from our negative experiences.

It is possible to take away a negative lesson from the situations we face in life. We can let betrayal teach us to never trust anyone again or we can let it teach us something that honors God and

His Word. God does not allow us to walk through betrayal so we can learn to stay away from people but so we can learn how to walk through life with people.

God also may use betrayal to teach you about yourself. When I walked through my first betrayal in ministry, I was devastated, but I sought the Lord so I would become better and not bitter. When a staff member betrayed me for the first time, I didn't expect to encounter the same emotions I felt after my first experience with betrayal. I thought those emotions had been conquered. I was very wrong. I had to ask God daily to help me keep my temper under control and my attitude right.

Betrayal also has taught me a lot about my wife. Jelly is only about five feet tall, but she can pack a wallop. One night I was in a meeting with one of the people who had come against my leadership in the church. The meeting had become pretty nasty. I was being baited and threatened over and over again. The door to our meeting room was closed, and that is usually a sign that no one is to enter. But all of a sudden the door burst open, and my wife was standing on the other side. I knew there was about to be a throw down by the way she looked at me and then at the person who was haranguing me.

To my knowledge Jelly has never beaten anyone up except during a college-wide pillow fight, but I could not take any chances that night. In retrospect it would have saved me some trouble had I let her deal with him—if I could have done that and kept her out of jail. In all seriousness Jelly did not get physically violent that night, but she caused me to remember how blessed I am to have a wife who would come so powerfully to my defense.

What we can learn from betrayal is as varied as the types of betrayal we may encounter. The lessons depend entirely on God and what He wants to teach us at that time in our lives. If we don't learn a lesson the first time, He will allow us to repeat the course. So while some lessons are learned after the first incident of betrayal, others may be repeated.

Wounded Warriors

Someone once said, "Out of suffering have emerged the strongest souls. The most massive characters are seared with scars."[2] When we talk about wounds and warriors, I think of our armed forces and the sacrifices US troops have made in the war on terror. They leave all that is familiar and go overseas to put their lives on the line for something they believe in. Some of those warriors come home and some do not.

Those who do return home are forever changed. Their injuries may be visible or invisible; often the emotional injuries are much worse and harder to heal than the physical wounds. Many of our soldiers come home with post-traumatic stress disorder (PTSD). For many years this was an ignored injury. Many soldiers who returned home with PTSD never received treatment and later committed suicide. Even now that there is greater awareness of PTSD, soldiers are still suffering. Suicide rates continue to climb throughout our military with 349 service members taking their lives in 2012, up 15 percent from the 301 suicides reported in 2011.[3] Emotional wounds are very real and can be deadly if not treated.

My dear friend Dave Roever was terribly wounded in Vietnam. He still bears disfiguring scars from a phosphorus grenade that blew up in his hand. He is one of the bravest men I know. Although he sustained life-threatening wounds in Vietnam, he has repeatedly traveled to that country to minister to the very people who once wanted to take his life. He visits our troops overseas every year, encouraging them and building morale. In Colorado he has built a ranch for wounded warriors where he works to reestablish their will and hope. Dave has been through multiple surgeries, skin grafts, and physical therapy. Despite all of that, physical scars remain, but his emotional and spiritual wounds are no longer open. Those wounds have been healed by the power of God, and He has made Dave into a great warrior with a cause.

In much the same way, God wants to heal us of the deep wounds of betrayal and make us into great warriors for His cause. The first step toward possessing this healing is to let go of the desire for revenge. Revenge destroys relationships, but forgiveness preserves relationships.

To exact revenge is to intentionally inflict hurt or harm on someone as punishment for a wrong that has been suffered. Although retaliation may feel sweet for a moment, it is not worth the heartache it will eventually cause you. If you listen to the dictates of our society, you will be made to feel that vengeance is your right. As followers of Christ, we do not live by the dictates of this society but by the precepts of God's Word. When you forgive, you let go of the idea that you have the right to retaliate. The Bible is clear about this:

> Vengeance is Mine, and recompense; their foot shall slip in due time; for the day of their calamity is at hand, and the things to come hasten upon them.
> —DEUTERONOMY 32:35

> Do not take revenge, my dear friends, but leave room for God's wrath, for it is written: "It is mine to avenge; I will repay," says the Lord.
> —ROMANS 12:19, NIV

I am not going to tell you to forgive and move on. That would be trite. Forgiveness is typically not easy. Most of the time it takes a good deal of time and effort, because it is a process. When you forgive, you are saying you are willing to make a fresh start. When you forgive, you are acknowledging that people are more important than their faults and betrayals. Forgiveness says you recognize that there is a need for grace.

That does not mean you condone a person's behavior or act as if the betrayal never occurred. Forgiveness does not deny that someone hurt you. In order to forgive, you must admit that you were wronged and accept the emotions associated with that realization. You should not minimize what happened to you or allow the betrayer to justify his or her behavior.

When you forgive, you recognize that a wrong has been done but you choose not to seek vengeance. You give up the desire to get even or punish them. Instead you are able to pray that God blesses them with a sincere heart. This is not for the other person's benefit but for yours. When someone has betrayed you and you choose to forgive them, a vertical exchange takes place between you and God. This exchange brings peace into your heart and frees God to bring about justice in whatever way He sees fit. Releasing the person who wronged you allows you to move past the victim mentality, which holds you hostage to the very thing you want to forget. Forgiveness frees you from reliving the pain every day, possibly even every moment of every day.

There was a line in a romantic movie from the seventies that became so popular it is now a cliché: "Love means never having to say you're sorry."[4] Not only was this saying trite, it was also untrue. Love means you have to say you are sorry over and over again. When you truly love someone, you live a life of forgiveness. Forgiveness is key to restoring and preserving relationships.

Some of the wisest, strongest men I have ever known have been deeply wounded. They became such great men because they allowed their wounds to heal and become scars. Scars are not reminders of past pain; they are an indication that you went through a difficult experience and lived to tell about it.

My pastor is my hero. He has been a pastor for more than forty years, spending more than thirty-five of those years at the same church. During the charismatic renewal of the 1970s, he became a great believer in faith. He preached about the power of faith and lived it. When his beautiful five-year-old daughter was diagnosed with cancer, he believed God would heal her. Every day he would look at the tumor protruding from the side of her face and neck and curse it, believing that she was already healed. Eventually, however, his daughter died.

My pastor did, said, lived, and preached all the right things, yet his daughter was not healed in the way he had hoped. For many months after her death he and his family were heart-broken, and they wondered if God had failed them or if He had betrayed their faith. But my pastor didn't stop there. He could have become bitter and given up on God but he didn't do that. He gave God all the hurt and pain and surrendered to His healing process. Because he did, my pastor is still loving others and making a tremendous impact in the kingdom today.

Mark and Huldah Buntain traveled to India in the late 1950s. They began a ministry to the people of Calcutta that grew larger than they ever imagined. When Mark Buntain slipped and fell one day, no one thought that within a few short hours he would be in the arms of the Lord. Huldah, a great woman of God, had a choice to make. She could finish the work they had started or go home dreaming of what could have been. She chose to stay in Calcutta and expand the ministry and realize the dreams God had given her and Mark. To date twenty-five thousand children are fed, educated, and medically assisted every day through their ministry. More than seven hundred churches have been birthed, a nursing school and public hospital have been built, and multiple souls have been won to the kingdom. This happened because one wounded woman became a warrior. She chose to release any anger or bitterness she may have felt toward God and let the Holy Spirit heal her. Because she did that, she was free to walk into all that God had for her.[5]

Don't Fear the Dark Times

Physical darkness is defined as the absence of light. One of the first things that God did when He created the earth was to separate the light and darkness.

> In the beginning God created the heavens and the earth. Now the earth was formless and empty, darkness was over the surface of the deep, and the Spirit of God was hovering over the waters. And God said, "Let there be light," and there was light.
> —GENESIS 1:1–3, NIV

In addition to physical darkness there is also spiritual and emotional darkness represented by Satan and sin. Part of the pain of betrayal is caused by the emotional darkness that can begin to permeate our lives. We see no light at the end of the proverbial tunnel. The darkness is so deep we're not sure what step will take us in the right direction.

Many people are afraid of the dark. The reasons for this are as varied as the people and their personalities. The most obvious reason for fear of the dark is that we can't see what's out there.

If you do not know what is out there, you cannot defend yourself. You may even imagine things that are not there, such as the boogeyman.

Imagine you are in a public setting one evening when the power goes out. You can hear almost everyone in the room taking a deep breath. Someone yells, "Don't move. You could get hurt!" Then someone else yells, "I am getting out of here!" Pandemonium breaks out until someone finds a match, a lighter, or a flashlight to provide a little light.

Emotional darkness evokes some of the same feelings as physical darkness does, namely fear of the unknown. You may wonder, "What will happen as a result of this betrayal?" "Will I ever get through it?" "How will I defend myself?" "How long will I feel this way?" Or you may imagine things. The betrayer may become larger than life, and you may think he or she has more power than you do, is stronger than you are, and can do more damage than you know. Once you begin to see a little light in the darkness, the situation may not seem as bad as it did at first.

The apostle Paul said there would be times when we could not see clearly and would see only part of what God has in store for us.

> For we know in part and we prophesy in part. But when that which is perfect has come, then that which is in part will be done away.
> When I was a child, I spoke as a child, I understood as a child, I thought as a child; but when I became a man, I put away childish things. For now we see in a mirror, dimly, but then face to face. Now I know in part, but then I shall know just as I also am known.
> —1 CORINTHIANS 13:9–12

God will reveal everything in time. He does not reveal every-thing about our lives to us as soon as we ask Him to do so. He reveals a little at a time, teaching us and training us so we can receive His plans. When it's sunny outside and then suddenly gets darker, we often say the sun went behind a cloud. That is not actually true. The sun went nowhere. It was the cloud that moved and blocked the sun's rays. Only when that cloud moves again will we have an unimpeded view of the sun.

God never moves. He never puts you in darkness. He some-times allows cloudy circumstances to come your way and block your view, but when the cloud moves, you will again see Him at work in your life. When you take God's Word and apply it to your life, you will become steadfast and unmovable. Your determination to pursue God will take you to your next step. If you have been betrayed, grieve for the relationship that has been damaged or even lost, but keep moving forward toward healing.

Betrayal Can Produce Humility

I have learned from experience that humbling and even humili-ating circumstances can bring us to a place of humility before God. When someone sends your entire congregation a twenty-six-page document on what a rotten person you are, you wonder how many people believe the lies in the document. You watch people to see if they are talking about you. You are almost afraid to answer the telephone and hear someone else criticize you. You also begin to wonder if there is a thread of truth in anything that was said.

Let me address something: taking a moment for self-reflection is not a bad thing. When someone makes an accusation against you, rather than becoming defensive, it is good to become introspective. Is there something you need to change or that you could do better? Are you sending the wrong messages with your body language? When you have answered those questions honestly to the best of your ability, you can allow the Holy Spirit to begin the healing process in your heart. When your conscience is clear before God, you can let Him work on your attitude. Sometimes we have to look backward and inward in order to move forward.

When we are dealing with betrayal, we often get grace, mercy, and justice mixed up. Justice says, "You deserve this." We all want God to be full of justice where other people are concerned, especially when they hurt us. Grace, however, is defined as unmerited favor. It says, "You don't deserve this but you can have it anyway."

Not one of us deserves what Jesus Christ did for us on the cross. We could never merit that kind of sacrifice, but He didn't need us to deserve it. He gave us His life because He loved us. People who betray do not deserve grace, but situations of betrayal give us an opportunity to extend grace to them. Grace does not absolve the person of wrongdoing; it just lets them know that you are willing to forgive.

While justice says, "You deserve this," and grace says, "You don't deserve this but you can have it anyway," mercy says, "You deserve this, but you are not getting it." Mercy works toward canceling someone's debt. We deserve to be punished for our sins, but because of God's mercy toward us we will not get what we deserve. We are to operate with grace toward others, especially those who have despitefully used us. When we reach out with grace, mercy follows, and God takes care of the justice.

Battling betrayal is not a one-time event. Unfortunately we

will face this battle more often in life than we would like. But we can win the fight and through our example show others how to do the same. The ball is in your court. I encourage you to choose to be an overcomer!

Chapter 11

DON'T LOOK BACK

'VE HEARD PEOPLE say they would like to be in their twenties again. Not me! If I could turn back time, knowing all that I know now, I would do some things differently. But I would never want to repeat the past, learning the same lessons from the same circumstances. Hindsight is 20/20, and we can all see more clearly when we are looking back. But the big question is, do you want to spend your life thinking about what was, could have been, or should have been? Or do you want to live a life without regrets?

When you are traveling, one of the fastest ways to get motion sickness is to not focus on the horizon in front of you. My wife and children do not like road trips. It could have something to do with my driving. When I get behind the wheel of a car, my competitive spirit takes over. No one is going to pass me or go faster than me. If we stop for a bathroom break, when I get back on the road, I want to pass the same people all over again.

If we are going on a long trip, Jelly will put in her ear phones, cover her head, and listen to music. She says if she's going to die, she does not want to see it coming. She wants it to be a surprise. Our girls do not do this. They will play games on their phones, work on their laptops, maybe read a book. Before long one of them is yelling, "Quick, pull over!" When you hear those words, you know somebody is going to be sick, and it is in your best interest to do exactly as they ask and pull over quickly.

Recently Jelly and I took our children, son-in-law, and grand-daughter to an out-of-town funeral. The wind was fierce, and the car was swaying like an old-fashioned roller coaster. We had been on the road for about an hour when I heard the distressed call from the back. I couldn't get over fast enough, so my daughter got sick in her drink cup. When her sisters smelled it, they got sick in their drink cups as well.

As soon as I was able to pull the car over, the girls piled out, losing what was left in their stomachs as they went. At least that was what they were supposed to do: lose it outside of the car. But by the time they were all on the side of the road, the daughter who started the fuss told me she could not be sick in front of strangers (the people who were driving by). So I had one sick daughter who couldn't be sick, another doubled over, and a third just getting a breath of fresh air. Jelly was taking pictures of the whole thing, laughing all the while. We spent a good five minutes just laughing at the situation on the side of the road. (Of course, I had to make up that time when everyone piled back into the car.)

Later my know-it-all wife informed me that the wind was not blowing but that I had a bad tire. Life is never dull.

When you are in a moving car, the potential for motion sickness is high if you don't keep your eyes on what's in front of you. In a similar way, when you focus on what is behind you while journeying through life, the potential for "e-motion" sickness is very high. We begin to regret times when we failed or things that we've lost, and we can get stuck in that place if we're not careful.

God did not design us to spend our lives looking at the past. That is one of Satan's tricks—to get us to look behind and not focus on the present or the future. Maybe that is why the apostle Paul told us to forget those things behind us:

> Not that I have already obtained all this, or have already arrived at my goal, but I press on to take hold of that for which Christ Jesus took hold of me. Brothers and sisters, I do not consider myself yet to have taken hold of it. But one thing I do: Forgetting what is behind and straining toward what is ahead, I press on toward the goal to win the prize for which God has called me heavenward in Christ Jesus.
> —PHILIPPIANS 3:12–14, NIV

The past is over, and we cannot change anything about it. We can do something about the future, but not if we are living in the past. Many of us have heard stories of the way it used to be. It is OK to be nostalgic and reminisce occasionally. It is OK to tell the stories about the past so our children and grandchildren know their history. But to wallow in the past, ruminating about mistakes made and missed opportunities will do you no good.

I know a man who emigrated from Southeast Asia to the United States many years ago. Whenever I am sitting across a table from him, I ask him to tell me a story of his war days. He is always more than willing to comply. He tells of blowing up bridges when he was twelve years old and hiding from Japanese soldiers. He has told me many stories over the years, and I never tire of hearing them. As he shares his stories I think of how God has protected him and all that the Lord has done in and through him. He does not live in the past. His past informs the future; it does not replace it.

We are to be lifelong learners. Once we learn a skill, we are to move on and learn something new. When you have learned how to recognize a betrayer and how to deal with him, you are supposed to move on. That does not mean you will never experience another betrayal, but it does mean you are not to take the pain of past betrayals into the future.

Betrayal is not the end of the road. It may look like the end. You may want it to be the end, but it is just another bend in your journey through life. In 2012 Jelly and I decided we were going to visit California and drive down the coastal highway from San Francisco to San Diego. It is one of the most scenic drives in America. Every vista is more beautiful than the last; every bend brings a beautiful new surprise. One of the things I love most about the drive is that there are so many places to pull over and enjoy the scenery. When you see one of these stops, you will probably miss something if you do not pull over.

While most of the stops are designed to allow travelers to enjoy the scenery, others are there for emergencies—a truck whose brakes have gotten too hot or someone with a flat tire...or motion sickness. In life you may have to occasionally pull over to enjoy the scenery or to rest. If you do not pull over, you may miss something that God has designed just for you. You may miss a lesson or an opportunity to help someone else who is facing a similar trial.

Pulling over is also critical in emergency situations. If life gets too hot, you may get into an accident if you try to continue. Life may seem out of balance because your emotions are being tossed around. When this happens you know that you need to check your equipment to see if your attitude—your spirit—is still in line with God's Word. To not stop and rest or to not stop to cool down or check the equipment is foolish. This is when you will go over the side of the mountain, wounding or killing yourself and others in the vicinity.

Become a Wounded Healer

With each challenge we face, there will be something to learn. When we begin to look at betrayal as a learning experience, we will see that the lesson is not just for our own benefit. It is for us to help others. You may not feel like helping others. You may not even want to help others because the pain is so very raw. Rest assured, there will come a time in life when God will call on you to hold out your hand to someone who is walking through a betrayal. God will want you to tell that person that you have been there, felt their pain, and, most importantly, survived.

In 2005 our oldest daughter, Jordan, was engaged to a young man in our church. After a brief illness, Bruce died, and she was left devastated by her loss. We walked her through the tragedy, trying to help her become healthy and whole again. She did not want to hear that God was going to use her circumstance to help someone else, but she knew in her heart that was true.

The spring after Bruce's death, I received a call from a missionary whose daughter had been tragically killed just three weeks before her wedding. They wanted to know if Jordan could please reach out to their late daughter's fiancé and try to help him walk through the early stages of his pain. Jordan was more than happy to do so. I was never a part of their conversations, but I did have the opportunity to meet the young man months afterward, and he was so very grateful for her help.

Later that same spring one of Jordan's childhood friends lost her husband in a boating accident. When I received the call to come to the hospital, Jordan wanted to go with me. I did not think it was a good idea because Jordan's loss was still so fresh. I will never forget her response as she said, "Dad, I have to go. I am the only one who will be there that knows what she is going through." I knew then that not only would she go to the hospital, but also she would minister to her friend and was on her way to becoming a wounded healer.

That is what God wants for all of us. When we walk through heartache, we are to take the knowledge and understanding we gain and use it to help someone else. It becomes a tool for ministry that we have purchased with our own pain. Tools are good when they are used for the purpose for which they were designed, but they do no good hanging in a closet or lying in a toolbox, hidden away for no one to use. Use the tools you gain from betrayal to help others.

When you begin to reach out to others in pain, it shifts your focus. You do not think as much about your own heartache; you think about how to help others walk through theirs. You become a wounded healer.

Have you ever been a part of a class that is based on theory— a physics, sociology, or psychology course, perhaps? A theory is a body of rules, ideas, principles, and techniques that are applied to a practice. The theory may have never been applied, but it sounds good. A person can teach musical theory without knowing how to actually play an instrument. Someone can teach you about fund-raising, but if that person has never been successful at raising funds, you will probably not follow their techniques. When you reach out to someone who is reeling from a betrayal and you tell them that you have been there and done that and no longer wince from the pain of the wound, they are much more likely to listen to you than someone who has never faced a betrayal.

When the United States experienced an economic slowdown, many people in our church and our town faced great loss. Our economic base was in the airline and automotive industries. As the economy worsened and those industries began to fail, the finances of our church members suffered greatly. One day as she was reading the newspaper, Jelly counted eleven pages of foreclosures in our town alone. We lost two manufacturing companies, and unemployment rose to almost 18 percent.

In one week five millionaires came to me and said they were losing all of their financial assets and were going to be bankrupt. I gave them all the same advice: be faithful to God and He will see you through. Two of those individuals listened but three did not. The ones who listened avoided financial ruin; the other three suffered tremendous loss and are very bitter.

God wants us to honor Him even when it's hard. He wants us to praise and worship Him even when we do not feel like it. We are supposed to praise Him in the good times and the bad. According to the Merriam-Webster dictionary, the word *praise* means "to say or write good things about (someone or something), to express approval of (someone or something), or to express thanks to or love and respect for (God)."[1] By praising God, we ascribe value to Him. We are saying that there is value in the object of our worship and that our relationship with Him is important. Praise shifts our focus to the thing we value. Praising God causes us to focus on Him instead of the problem.

Of course, it is easier to praise God when things are going well than when we are facing difficulties in life. But the Bible doesn't say we are to praise God only when life is good. If you praised your children or valued your spouse only when they were pleasing you, your relationship with them would not be very healthy or strong. You value and love them for who they are, not merely for the good things they do for you.

The psalmist said:

> Enter his gates with thanksgiving and his courts with praise; give thanks to him and praise his name. For the LORD is good and his love endures forever; his faithfulness continues through all generations
>
> —PSALM 100:4–5, NIV

We are to praise God, regardless of the circumstances. Both good and bad things come our way. We are to praise and worship Him during both times—because He is good, His love endures forever, and He is faithful throughout the ages.

In 1955 Hannah Hurnard published an allegory titled *Hinds' Feet on High Places*. It is the story of a girl, Much-Afraid Fearing, who wants to become a mature believer and walk in the high places of joy. In order to get into the high places, Much-Afraid must be guided by her two companions, Suffering and Sorrow. The book is filled with powerful insights, but I think this is one of the most incredible. Too often we think we can become mature believers without ever having to endure any suffering or sorrow. How can we know the heights of joy unless we have also experienced the depths of suffering and sorrow?

The Bible says:

> The Sovereign LORD is my strength; he makes my feet like the feet of a deer, he enables me to tread on the heights.
>
> —HABAKKUK 3:19, NIV

God Is Merciful and Mighty

I would be remiss if I did not mention Job as we talk about walking through betrayal. He was an amazing man who understood that God was both merciful and mighty.

> One day when Job's sons and daughters were feasting and drinking wine at the oldest brother's house, a messenger came to Job and said, "The oxen were plowing and the donkeys were grazing nearby, and the Sabeans attacked and made off with them. They put the servants to the sword, and I am the only one who has escaped to tell you!"
>
> While he was still speaking, another messenger came and said, "The fire of God fell from the heavens and burned up the sheep and the servants, and I am the only one who has escaped to tell you!"
>
> While he was still speaking, another messenger came and said, "The Chaldeans formed three raiding parties and swept down on your camels and made off with them. They put the servants to the sword, and I am the only one who has escaped to tell you!"
>
> While he was still speaking, yet another messenger came and said, "Your sons and daughters were feasting and drinking wine at the oldest brother's house, when suddenly a mighty wind swept in from the desert and struck the four corners of the house. It collapsed on them and they are dead, and I am the only one who has escaped to tell you!"
>
> At this, Job got up and tore his robe and shaved his head. Then he fell to the ground in worship and said: "Naked I came from my mother's womb, and naked I will

depart. The LORD gave and the LORD has taken away; may the name of the LORD be praised."

In all this, Job did not sin by charging God with wrongdoing.

—Job 1:13–22, NIV

Job recognized that everything he had came from God and that he was only a steward of God's blessings. Even in his pain Job gave God glory: "The LORD gave and the LORD has taken away; may the name of the LORD be praised" (v. 21). The Sabeans came and carried off Job's oxen and donkey. The fire of God burned up the sheep and the servants. The Chaldeans took away his camels, yet Job does not castigate God. When all of his children were killed, Job simply said that the God who gave them to him has the right to take them.

In the midst of Job's physical pain and suffering, his wife challenged him to curse God and die. He responded by telling her, "Shall we accept good from God, and not trouble?" (Job 2:10). Job shows in his response that he is a man who can accept good things from God as well as trouble. Job knew it was not his own effort that produced blessings.

Whatever your theology may be about Job, there is one thing we can all agree on: Job kept a right attitude that allowed God to work on his behalf!

And so it was, after the LORD had spoken these words to Job, that the LORD said to Eliphaz the Temanite, "My wrath is aroused against you and your two friends, for you have not spoken of Me what is right, as My servant Job has. Now therefore, take for yourselves seven bulls and seven rams, go to My servant Job, and offer up for yourselves a burnt offering; and My servant Job shall pray for you. For I will accept him, lest I deal with you according to your folly; because you have not spoken of Me what is right, as My servant Job has."

So Eliphaz the Temanite and Bildad the Shuhite and Zophar the Naamathite went and did as the Lord commanded them; for the LORD had accepted Job. And the LORD restored Job's losses when he prayed for his friends. Indeed the LORD gave Job twice as much as he had before. Then all his brothers, all his sisters, and all those who had been his acquaintances before, came to him and ate food with him in his house; and they consoled him and comforted him for all the adversity that the LORD had brought upon him. Each one gave him a piece of silver and each a ring of gold.

Now the LORD blessed the latter days of Job more than his beginning; for he had fourteen thousand sheep, six thousand camels, one thousand yoke of oxen, and one thousand female donkeys. He also had seven sons and three daughters. And he called the name of the first Jemimah, the name of the second Keziah, and the name of the third Keren-Happuch. In all the land were found no women so beautiful as the daughters of Job; and their father gave them an inheritance among their brothers.

After this Job lived one hundred and forty years, and saw his children and grandchildren for four generations. So Job died, old and full of days.

—Job 42:7–17

Job had friends who tried to comfort him during his crisis, but they managed to blame him for the hardship he was experiencing. They accused Job of betraying God. They were so wrong in their assessment of the situation that God became angry and instructed them to offer a sacrifice and to ask Job to pray for them. It was only after he prayed for his friends that God brought complete restoration to Job. The Bible does not tell us that Job refused to pray for them or refused their gifts. Job kept his attitude right and freely offered both prayer and hospitality to those who had accused him of having done something sinful to warrant the pain he was facing.

I don't know about you, but the hardest thing for me when I have faced betrayal is to keep my attitude and heart right before God. When my attitude is wrong, I confess my sins because God is faithful to forgive me of my sins and cleanse me (1 John 1:9). He will wipe all my sins away as if they never existed.

Praise Your Way to Victory

Psalm 149 tells us how to praise our way through to victory when we have been betrayed.

> Let his faithful people rejoice in this honor and sing for joy on their beds. May the praise of God be in their mouths and a double-edged sword in their hands, to inflict vengeance on the nations and punishment on the peoples, to bind their kings with fetters, their nobles with shackles of iron, to carry out the sentence written against them—this is the glory of all his faithful people. Praise the LORD.
>
> —PSALM 149:5–9, NIV

Our worship is never more pure before the Lord than when we praise Him in the midst of difficult circumstances. When we praise Him, we are refusing to play the role of a victim, because we are acknowledging that God is still in control, and He always wins. Praising God turns our attention to God's goodness and His ability to do exceedingly abundantly above all that we could ask or think (Eph. 3:20). God is then able to create a miracle out of the mess a betrayal has caused in our lives or organizations, because our worship puts us in communion with the divine being who created our souls and knows exactly how to heal it!

Praise and worship releases supernatural faith into your heart as you walk through betrayal. It helps you see that God is more than able to take care of the situation—and to take care of you through the situation. Worship becomes an impenetrable wall against doubt, fear, and unbelief.

It has been said that we must chart our course before the storm hits. When you are going through the difficulties of life you must draw strength from your relationship with God. In times of crisis you depend on the things you are sure of! Knowing your course means you know God's character, His Word, and His attributes. It means you know He will bring you through the circumstance.

When you are under spiritual assault, your worship may need to become *war-ship*. Your worship may need to become a battle cry. You may need to press in to the presence of God and go to war about the situation. You may be reeling from spiritual blows leveled against you, but that is when you must praise God even more. Praise and worship are weapons of mass destruction against the enemy.

There comes a time in all of our lives when we have to decide if we are going to live for Jesus Christ regardless of the situation, the pain, the heartache, or the sorrow. We must declare that we will remain faithful to our Savior no matter what comes our way. We are not to be controlled by our circumstances or our heartaches. Our faith and commitment must be steadfast.

Horatio G. Spafford made his statement of faith through the words of a song. He and his family had lived through the great Chicago fire of 1871. For two years he assisted in helping the people of Chicago recover from the trauma. Needing a vacation, he sent his wife and four daughters ahead of him to England. The *SS Ville du Havre* collided with another ship and sank within twenty minutes. His wife survived by clinging to a piece of wreckage. When she arrived in Wales, she telegraphed her husband, "Saved alone. What shall I do..."[2]

Horatio Spafford immediately rushed to the side of his grief-stricken wife. As Horatio's ship passed the place where his children had died, he went to his cabin and penned these words:

> When peace, like a river, attendeth my way,
> When sorrows like sea billows roll;
> Whatever my lot, Thou has taught me to say,
> It is well, it is well, with my soul.
>
> Though Satan should buffet, though trials should come,
> Let this blest assurance control,
> That Christ has regarded my helpless estate,
> And hath shed His own blood for my soul.
>
> My sin, oh, the bliss of this glorious thought!
> My sin, not in part but the whole,
> Is nailed to the cross, and I bear it no more,
> Praise the Lord, praise the Lord, O my soul!
>
> For me, be it Christ, be it Christ hence to live:
> If Jordan above me shall roll,
> No pang shall be mine, for in death as in life
> Thou wilt whisper Thy peace to my soul.
>
> But, Lord, 'tis for Thee, for Thy coming we wait,
> The sky, not the grave, is our goal;

Oh trump of the angel! Oh voice of the Lord!
Blessed hope, blessed rest of my soul!

And Lord, haste the day when my faith shall be sight,
The clouds be rolled back as a scroll;
The trump shall resound, and the Lord shall descend,
Even so, it is well with my soul.[3]

Are you sure your relationship with Christ is strong enough to see you through betrayal? You can have the assurance of a strong relationship with Jesus Christ. It is not difficult, but it is humbling. Have you simply said, "Jesus, help me"? This is a simple prayer to an almighty God who brings amazing and profound results. Jesus has promised to never leave us or forsake us. He has never and will never leave us; therefore, we can seek God in prayer, knowing He is listening.

Why not invite God into your dilemma? Why not humble yourself before Him and bow in worship?

If you praise God through your trial, He will lead and guide you every step of the way. He will heal your heart and enable you to help others. He will remove the brokenness and bitterness and give you an education that will empower you to exalt the name of the Lord and bring destruction to the works of Satan. Your healing is only a prayer away. Ask Jesus to help you heal. You will be glad you did!

You can survive betrayal. You can even become better as a result of it. Keep your focus on the Lord and not on your pain or on those who betrayed you. Trust Him and He will see you through.

Dear Jesus, protect my heart from bitterness and unforgiveness. I submit my will and emotions freely to You and the Holy Spirit, and to the authority of the

Word of God. I ask that You override the weakness of my flesh that would prohibit me in any way from doing what You have called me to do. Help me walk in healing, deliverance, and restoration. I claim, according to Your Word, that the betrayal I have experienced will not lead to defeat but be a pathway to maturity and blessing. I also pray that You will give me the wisdom and strength to share these truths You have taught me to bless Your kingdom and others I come in contact with. As You said in Your Word, the truth will set me free. Thank You for Your truth. Today is the first day of total freedom from betrayal's bitterness. By faith I thank You for this, in Jesus's name. Amen.

NOTES

Introduction

1. Sharon Jacobs, "Chemical Warfare, From Rome to Syria. A Time Line." *National Geographic*, August 22, 2013, http://news .nationalgeographic.com/news/2013/08/130822-syria-chemical -biological-weapons-sarin-war-history-science/ (accessed February 12, 2014).

2. John W. Fountain, "Notre Dame Coach Resigns After 5 Days and a Few Lies, *The New York Times*, December 15, 2001, http://www.nytimes.com/2001/12/15/sports/notre-dame-coach -resigns-after-5-days-and-a-few-lies.html (accessed February 12, 2014).

3. Biography.com, "Bernard Madoff," http://www.biography .com/people/bernard-madoff-466366?page=2 (accessed February 12, 2014).

4. Linda L. Creighton, "Benedict Arnold: A Traitor, but Once a Patriot," *US News & World Report*, June 27, 2008, http://www .usnews.com/news/national/articles/2008/06/27/benedict-arnold-a -traitor-but-once-a-patriot (accessed February 12, 2014); Biography .com, "Benedict Arnold," http://www.biography.com/people/ benedict-arnold-9189320?page=1 (accessed February 12, 2014).

Chapter 1
The Genesis of Betrayal

1. W. K. McNeil, ed., *Encyclopedia of American Gospel Music* (New York: Routledge, 2010), 303.

2. Ibid., 283.

3. Steven Otfinoski, *African Americans in the Performing Arts* (New York: Facts on File, Inc., 2003), 106.

4. Wikipedia.org, "Little Richard," http://en.wikipedia.org/wiki/Little_Richard#cite_ref-Britannica_21-0 (accessed February 12, 2014).

Chapter 2
The Ten Commandments: God's Protection From Betrayal

1. Abort73.com, "U.S. Abortion Statistics," http://www.abort73.com/abortion_facts/us_abortion_statistics/ (accessed February 12, 2014).

2. James Tillman, "New Report Suggests Over 1 Billion Abortions Committed: Pro-Life Activists," Lifesitenews.com, October 16, 2009, http://www.lifesitenews.com/ldn/2009/oct/09101604.html (accessed February 12, 2014).

3. *Huffington Post*, "Cheating Wives on the Rise," July 3, 2013, http://www.huffingtonpost.com/2013/07/02/cheating-wives_n_3536412.html (accessed February 12, 2014).

4. H. R. Jerajani, Bhagyashri Jaju, M. M. Phiske, and Nitin Lade, "Hematidrosis—A Rare Clinical Phenomenon," *Indian Journal of Dermatology* 54, no. 3 (July-September 2009): 290–292, http://www.ncbi.nlm.nih.gov/pmc/articles/PMC2810702/ (accessed February 12, 2014); Lee Strobel, "What You're Missing From the Lee Strobel 'Investigating Faith' newsletter," April 4, 2011, http://www.biblegateway.com/blog/2011/04/what-youre-missing-from-the-lee-strobel-newsletter/ (accessed February 12, 2014).

Chapter 3
Guard Your Heart

1. Adrian Rogers, in communication with the author, 2005.

2. Courtenay Smith and Alison Caporimo, "Reader's Digest Trust Poll: Why Do We Trust at All?", *Reader's Digest*, June 2013.

Chapter 4
How to Identify a Betrayer

1. As heard by the author at a missions conference.

2. Fred H. Wright, "Manners and Customs of Bible Lands," http://tinyurl.com/k5sb3av (accessed February 12, 2014).

Chapter 10
The Benefits of Betrayal

1. YouTube.com, "Big Girls Falls Backwards Off the Table While Singing!!", https://www.youtube.com/watch?v=fv_Ey -XOkZU (accesed March 19, 2014).
2. Thinkexist.com, "Kahlil Gibran Quotes," http://thinkexist .com/quotation/out_of_suffering_have_emerged_the_strongest_ souls/259185.html (accessed February 13, 2014).
3. RT.com, "US Military Suicides Continue to Climb, Reaching Record in 2012," http://www.rt.com/usa/us-army-suicide-rate-025/ (accessed March 19, 2014); Bill Briggs, "Military Suicide Rate Hit Record High in 2012," NBC News, January 14, 2013, http://usnews .nbcnews.com/_news/2013/01/14/16510852-military-suicide-rate-hit -record-high-in-2012?lite (accessed March 19, 2014).
4. *Love Story*, directed by Arthur Hiller (Los Angeles: Paramount Pictures, 1970).
5. Calcutta Mercy Ministries, "Our History," http://www .buntain.org/who-we-are/our-history (accessed January 7, 2014); see also *Awaken*, Calcutta Mercy Ministries, 2013.

Chapter 11
Don't Look Back

1. Merriam-Webster.com, s.v. "praise," http://www.merriam -webster.com/dictionary/praise (accessed April 1, 2014).
2. Library of Congress, "The American Colony in Jerusalem: Family Tragedy," http://www.loc.gov/exhibits/americancolony/ amcolony-family.html (accessed February 13, 2014).
3. "It Is Well With My Soul" by Horatio G. Spafford. Public domain.

WWW.GRIFFINFIRST.ORG

EMPOWERED
TO RADICALLY CHANGE
YOUR WORLD

FREE NEWSLETTERS
TO HELP EMPOWER YOUR LIFE

Why subscribe today?

❏ **DELIVERED DIRECTLY TO YOU.** All you have to do is open your inbox and read.

❏ **EXCLUSIVE CONTENT.** We cover the news overlooked by the mainstream press.

❏ **STAY CURRENT.** Find the latest court rulings, revivals, and cultural trends.

❏ **UPDATE OTHERS.** Easy to forward to friends and family with the click of your mouse.

CHOOSE THE E-NEWSLETTER THAT INTERESTS YOU MOST:

- Christian news
- Daily devotionals
- Spiritual empowerment
- And much, much more

SIGN UP AT: **http://freenewsletters.charismamag.com**

8178